Temporal and Eternal

CHARLES PÉGUY

Temporal and Eternal

CHARLES PÉGUY

Translated by Alexander Dru

Foreword by Pierre Manent

LIBERTY FUND

Clio I © 1931 and *Notre Jeunesse* © 1933 Editions Gallimard
Temporal and Eternal © 1958 Harvill Press
Foreword © 2001 Liberty Fund, Inc.
All rights reserved
Printed in the United States of America

Frontispiece courtesy of Corbis-Bettman.

| 10 | 21 | 22 | 23 | 24 | C | 6 | 5 | 4 | 3 | 2 |
| 21 | 22 | 23 | 24 | 25 | P | 6 | 5 | 4 | 3 | 2 |

Library of Congress Cataloging-in-Publication Data
Péguy, Charles, 1873–1914.
[Deuxième élégie XXX. English. Selections]
Temporal and eternal / Charles Péguy ; translated by Alexander Dru.
p. cm.
"An adaptation of Notre jeunesse (1910) and Clio I, which appeared in
the volume of inédits, Deuxième élégie XXX, 1955" — Prelim. p.
Includes bibliographical references.
ISBN 0-86597-321-0 (hardcover : alk. paper) —
ISBN 0-86597-322-9 (pbk. : alk. paper)
I. Dru, Alexander.   II. Title.
PQ2631.E25 D4813   2001
844'.912 — dc21   2001018794

Liberty Fund, Inc.
11301 N. Meridian Street
Carmel, Indiana 46032

An adaptation of

NOTRE JEUNESSE, *1910*

and of

CLIO I

which appeared in the volume of Inédits

DEUXIÈME ÉLÉGIE XXX, 1955

Contents

Foreword

It is difficult for an American reader not only to understand but even to gain access to the thinking of an author like Charles Péguy. We French can say that he was a great poet and a deep critic and thinker. But how can we give an idea of his greatness when nearly everything he wrote about is buried deep in French history, when everything he wrote seems to be essentially linked to an explicitly French perspective? How can we have Charles Péguy rise from the footnotes of scholarly studies of French history, or at most of the "European nation-state"?

The European nation-state is an object of pressing interest for every political animal — that is, for each of us, because it is the political form in which for better or worse we all live. It is indeed a contested and weakening form, but it is still the only real political entity we have. After all, the Soviet Union has reverted to its old national components. The United States is a prodigiously successful nation. And nobody knows whether the European Union, the greatest attempt to officially and decisively overcome the national basis of political life, will succeed gloriously, or collapse ignominiously.

At the time of Péguy's life, the European nation-states were basking in the sun of overweening glory while teetering on the brink of ignominy. They were busy building empires; educating the masses; cultivating the arts and sciences on a grand scale; and savoring, in English, French, or German, European man's finest hour. They were also about to enter the hellish cauldron of the First World War, whence all the evils of the century of evil would issue. Péguy died in the first weeks of the war, on the eve of the Battle of the Marne, as he led his platoon for an assault in the open. He was last heard shouting to his men, "For God's sake, push ahead!"

For centuries European peoples had lived a colorful and vibrant but hardly coherent life in the maze of their innumerable religious and secular institutions. For a long time ours was a checkered garment. We at last found the coherence of a common life in the framework of the nation-state, in which all the contents of human life merged. We found unity and community in the unity of our respective nations.

Those political and spiritual mergers were no harmonious pageants, no unanimous ceremonies. They involved forceful, and at times violent, measures. As every nation tried to form itself into the only true mystical body, it had to deal with mighty contenders. It would be a simplification, but perhaps an illuminating one, to say that the two mightiest contenders were, in very different, and even opposite, fashions, the Catholic Church on the one hand and the Jewish people on the other hand: the most visible and the least visible non-national communities in Europe at the time.

The Protestant churches had struck an early peace with the nations of which they were henceforth a part. Only the Catholic Church stuck to its self-understanding of being the *respublica perfecta*, the most and only perfect community.

In France, the conflict between the new nation and the old church took on a classical intensity and clarity. At the end of the nineteenth and the beginning of the twentieth century, after years of tumultuous confrontation, the nation, in the form of the eager and ambitious République, at last won the day and submitted the church to a definitive demotion through promulgating laws rigorously separating church and state. As the conflict between the republic and the church was coming to a head, the Dreyfus Affair broke out. This "immortal affair," as Péguy called it, was a cause célèbre for the whole world. After Captain Dreyfus, a French officer of the general staff, of Jewish descent, was falsely accused of treason, of having spied for Germany, the whole country was split into two irreconcilable camps, the camp of "Dreyfusards," composed mainly of republicans, and the camp of "Anti-Dreyfusards," composed principally of Catholics.

The emancipation of Jews through their integration into secular society and the state had brought about new problems as it solved old ones. Péguy was one of the first and most ardent Dreyfusards. In "Memories of Youth" (1910), he bitterly explains how, faithful to his original commitment and proud of it, he became disillusioned with most of his former companions, who had come to use the order of battle born from the Dreyfus Affair to take on the Catholic Church and submit it to a demeaning, illiberal political domination. In the course of this long, tortured process, Péguy went from being a socialist to becoming a Christian.

Because it generalizes and deepens the political bond, the modern nation-state tends to integrate the Jews and to absorb, or subjugate, the church, which excluded the Jews. But the official acceptance of the Jews into civil and even civic society is not necessarily synonymous with a true and genuine welcome. The Jews were invisible, or they were nowhere to be seen; now they are visible and thus, to some observers at least, they seem to be everywhere: in many Christian eyes, the modern nation-state, in France the modern République, which was subjugating the church, was but an instrument in the hands of the Jews, who have no nation, who are stateless. Today it is difficult to understand clearly this complex triangular debate in which the Catholics passionately identified themselves with half of the whole, the other half of which they rejected with an equal intensity: they saw themselves at one with this part of the modern nation-state, which they called "France," while they felt repugnance toward the other part, which was for them the "republic and the Jews." In the opposite camp, republicans tended to exclude Catholics from the "true" republic as they conceived it. France became the divided body whose travails paradoxically manifested the strength and the depth of the human longing for unity and wholeness. "To be a Jew," "to be a Frenchman," and "to be a Christian" were not only qualities, or identities, the compatibility of which both camps evaluated differently. They were also claims to the true whole as well as inchoate motions toward it. Thus, for Péguy the Dreyfus Affair was the meeting-point and the culmination of the history of France, the history of the Jewish people, and the history of Christianity. And the first "squad" of Dreyfusards, the only genuine ones, whom he called the "mystical body" of Dreyfusism, precisely embodied in the rarest fashion the three corresponding *mystiques:* the true Republic, the true

Christianity, and the true Israel were at one in their original decision for the innocence of Dreyfus.

To a contemporary reader, and in particular to an American one, what makes Péguy's treatment of the matter puzzling, and even foreign if not outlandish, is that the question of the community, and even of "communion," takes precedence over the question of individual rights. Not that he attributes to the community, religious or political, any rights over or against the rights of individual conscience: on that score, he is as liberal and even as anarchist as one can be. Otherwise, how could he have been among the first to side with the innocence of one man against the authority of the army in which the nation had rested its hopes? But once that juridical question is settled for him, it does not hold his attention. What interests him very much is the question of belonging, the question of the whole, or the wholes, to which we belong. You cannot solve that question through any shrewd adjudication of rights, separation of powers, or distribution of roles; you cannot solve it through theoretical analysis; you can solve it only through practical synthesis, that is, through a deepening of "belonging," a deepening of communion. Through his active participation in the Dreyfus Affair, Péguy deepened his understanding of what it means to be a Frenchman, to be a Jew, to be a Christian. There is no doubt, since he at last privately and publicly declared himself a Christian — refusing, it is true, his adhesion to the dogma of damnation — that he ended considering the Christian, particularly the Catholic, Church as the most complete and accordingly the truest communion. At the same time, he never ceased inveighing against the official, "bourgeois," church, never ceased preparing himself for the civic sacrifice as he saw the war coming, and never ceased deepening his personal and spiritual bond with the Jewish people.

If Péguy is susceptible to looking bizarre in our contemporary eyes, it is only because he was much more concrete and real than we ordinarily care to be. We dutifully and mechanically distinguish between private and public, between the individual and the community; and the distinction is valid as far as it goes. But how far does it go? Looking at Péguy's political and personal journey, we discover a spiritual triangle, the three poles of which are defined by three capital communities: the political or civic community, the Christian Church, and the Jewish people. If, tired of conventional discourse, we made a resolution to "get real," reading Péguy would be the right starting place.

PIERRE MANENT

Introduction

Although two volumes of Péguy's poetry have been published in English, his prose is only represented at the present time by two short "Selections" translated by Anne and Julian Green. His poetry is in fact much more accessible than his prose, in part because it is not embedded in the political feuds of the period, but also because it is more direct. The repetitions and variations which are tolerable in the form of free verse are not only more eccentric when presented as prose; they tend to increase and multiply and hold up or obscure the argument. And yet it could be maintained that Péguy was greater as a prose writer than as a poet. In any case Péguy's thought cannot be understood as long as his prose is ignored. With this in mind, I have tried to produce a readable version of two *Cahiers* which will form the first of three or four volumes covering the main body of his prose work.

The difficulty in translating Péguy's prose works lies in making them readable and intelligible without dehydrating the text to such an extent that it loses its quality. When M. Mauriac was told by Mr. Julian Green that he was translating *The Mystery of the Charity of Joan of Arc*, his comment was disconcerting. "What a pity," he remarked, "someone does not translate him into French." But no manipulation of the text, however ingenious, could make Péguy a correct writer. In France the problem has been solved to some extent by the publication of eleven or twelve volumes of *morceaux choisis,* the first of which, *Le Choix de Péguy,* was selected by Péguy himself, who may be presumed to have countenanced the method. This assumes, however, that Péguy's thought had, in the course of time, been assimilated and his ideas disseminated, as his influence spread. As this is not the case in England a different method seems to be called for.

It is largely for this reason that *Men and Saints* and *Basic Verities,* both of which are adroitly selected by Mr. Green, have made little impression. They are eminently readable, always short and self-contained. Inevitably, however, they fall into the genre of *pensées* and do not pretend to convey the characteristic elements of Péguy's work: the movement of his thought and his plodding gait. Without the repetitions and redundancies and the endless variations on a theme Péguy's peculiar method is lost. For these repetitions and the accompanying parenthesis, often more important than the thesis, are not merely a rhetorical device for hammering in home-truths. He can be very concise when he wishes.

"We are living at a period," Ballanche wrote in 1818, "when all ideas must be produced, and all the problems important to man must be expressed, at the same time. The feeling of simultaneity is the cause of the apparent incoherence which has been criticised in the [foregoing] prolegomena."

The problem which Ballanche raises in a rather naïve way is, in some respects, Péguy's. The thoughts which taken in isolation read like *pensées* are, properly speaking, fragments; the fragmentary method of composition so common to many of the romantic thinkers, such as Hamann, Novalis, Coleridge and Schlegel. It is erected into a principle in Kierkegaard's *Fragments of Philosophy*. Kierkegaard's work is also repetitive and he gloried in the number and elaboration of his parentheses, without bothering about the fact that it often makes him unreadable. But the repetitions serve a purpose, which is to present the "fragments" in a constantly varying and changing pattern. The "simultaneity," as Ballanche calls it, is the obverse of what in other thinkers is "the system": an indirect expression of the "whole" which cannot be expressed directly in a series of interlocking statements, because it cannot be known except fragmentarily, though the fragment must always consciously remain the obverse of the system. In that sense Péguy's method and style echo his conception of philosophy as a voyage of discovery, or, as he also calls it, a "system" of courage, in order to emphasize the central place of the paradox.

Therefore, this abridged translation of *Notre Jeunesse* and of the first version of *Clio* is not an attempt to tidy up his work and bring order into his thought, but rather the opposite; an attempt to preserve the order and emphasize the pattern. But I have, for example, suppressed the long digression on the Jews, with its tribute to Bernard Lazare, his close friend during the Dreyfus Affair, which forms a central part of the *Cahier* but destroys its balance. I have taken the same liberties with *Clio*, and in the second case have substantially curbed Péguy's style. My intention has not been to clip him into a recognized form, but to prune his style in order to reveal the fruit.

The choice of *Notre Jeunesse* and *Clio I* is dictated by the same reasons. There are other *Cahiers*, such as the *Note Con-*

jointe, which might have been translated with hardly any cuts. But there are none which go from a number of points simultaneously to the heart of Péguy's matter: Christianity in the modern world.

Notre Jeunesse was published in July, 1910, six months after *The Mystery of the Charity of Joan of Arc.* Some time in 1907 Joseph Reinach, one of the leading supporters of Dreyfus, suggested to Péguy that he should write an essay on the Affair. Péguy, who was incapable of writing to order, declined, but mentioned the suggestion to one of his closest friends and collaborators, Daniel Halévy. With Péguy's encouragement, though after a good deal of thought, Halévy agreed to write the history of the Dreyfus Affair and to publish it in the *Cahiers.* He realized that he was liable to offend the susceptibilities of some of his friends, but believed that after ten years or more had elapsed he could afford to treat his subject historically, and with Péguy's help went to work on *Apology for Our Past.* "How is it," he asked in all innocence, "that having felt so pleased with our Dreyfusism, or rather having taken such pride in it, how is it that today it arouses no more than a feeble response in us all?"

The *Apology* was published in the spring of 1910. Three months later Halévy was astonished to receive *Notre Jeunesse.* He had expected some replies, but he did not anticipate that the most violent would come from Péguy, taking him to task for writing in a penitent mood and for depreciating the rôle of Péguy's *Cahiers* during the Affair. From that time on, Halévy stopped attending the Thursday meetings at the offices of the *Cahiers* and only saw Péguy intermittently.

The origin of the first version of *Clio*, which I have called
Clio I for convenience, in order to distinguish it from the second version, *Clio: Dialogue de l'histoire et de l'âme paienne*,
is so far unknown. It was found among Péguy's papers and
appeared in 1955 with another unfinished work of little importance under a title which certainly preserves Péguy's tradition
of divorcing title from subject: *Deuxième élégie, XXX*. From
internal evidence it is clear that it must have been conceived
and in part written at the time that *Notre Jeunesse* filled his
mind. Not only are the themes the same, but *Clio I* develops
many of the ideas which occur for the first and only time in
Notre Jeunesse. Since 1907 Péguy had been bogged down in a
series of *Cahiers* on the place of history in the philosophy of
the modern world, of which three were published. Halévy's
book got him afloat again and he began *Clio I*. But before he
had finished it he was launched on a new series of *Cahiers*, and
instead of returning to the first version he entirely rewrote it
under the title given above. This second *Clio*, also unfinished,
was published shortly after his death.

Péguy's decision, if it was one, not to publish *Clio I* could be
accounted for on two grounds. In the first place, it is among the
most turgid of his works. And although self-criticism was not
his strongest suit, it is very possible that Péguy was anxious
not to endanger the success of *Notre Jeunesse* with a more than
usually characteristic text. It is also possible that he saw the
wisdom of not further antagonizing the Catholics with a violent attack on the clergy at a time when he still hoped that the
two sequels to *Joan of Arc*, *The Holy Innocents* and the *Porche*,
might establish his reputation as a Catholic writer. Moreover,
on reading *Notre Jeunesse*, Barrès had told him, somewhat in-

advisedly, that he ought to aim at the Academy, and Péguy, for the only time in his life, was optimistically grooming himself for success. Finally Bergson was being attacked by the Catholics and, though Péguy was not prepared to abandon Bergson, he was fully alive to the danger of exposing himself to further criticism on that score. His system of courage was for once wedded to prudence.

Many readers of *Notre Jeunesse* must have felt as amazed as Halévy at the violence with which Péguy took up the Dreyfus Affair when it had, at long last, become past history. To treat it as the turning point in the contemporary history of French politics and religion might seem like treating the Tichborne Case as the climax in the history of the British Empire and the spring of a Catholic revival.

Writing thirty years later, Halévy revised his views, and his excellent account of the background of *Notre Jeunesse* agrees at most points with Péguy's interpretation. The forces which Péguy had seen at work, and which his contemporaries could hardly distinguish, had in the meantime matured. He had claimed that the handful of independent supporters of Dreyfus represented by the *Cahiers* were not only in the right, ideally speaking, but that they alone had achieved anything. It could now be seen that this subjective and paradoxical view had in the interval been justified to some extent.

In 1910 it looked as though the Dreyfus Affair had deepened the rift in the French tradition beyond all repair. The conflict between Catholicism and the Republic was more bitter than ever before and even those who did not regard the opposition between the two camps as inevitable despaired of seeing any form of compromise or peace. That struggle had begun during the Revolution, when the attempt to build a national Church with a Civil Constitution for the clergy had been followed by a determined effort to wipe out Christianity. The excesses of the Revolution paved the way for the restoration of the Church in a propitious atmosphere, until the uncompromisingly clerical measures of 1828 once again created a breach in the nation. The outside observer in Péguy's day, even though not persuaded of any fundamental incompatability between Catholicism and the Revolution, could foresee no end to the struggle. Belloc, for example, had no solution to offer.

"The attempt to 'de-Christianize' France," he wrote in 1911, "failed, as I have said, completely. Public worship was restored and the Concordat of Napoleon was believed to have settled the relation between Church and State in a permanent fashion. We have lived to see it dissolved (1905), but this generation will not see, nor perhaps the generation succeeding it, the issue of the great struggle between two bodies of thought which are divided by no process of reason, but profoundly divorced by the action of vivid and tragic historical memories." [1]

Péguy's analysis of the situation, though it does not entirely contradict Belloc's, is utterly different. Both were agreed that Catholicism and the Revolution were not irreconcilable; but while Belloc attributed the great struggle to a divorce brought about by historical memories, Péguy held that the two bodies of thought had, in the course of time, evolved into ideologies which no longer corresponded to the faiths on which they were originally founded. The struggle had

1. *The French Revolution.* Home University Library, p. 252.

changed ground, and although the partisans still called themselves Catholics and Republicans, Catholicism and Republicanism had undergone a subtle change. In principle, they might not be divided by any process of reason; in fact, they adhered to doctrines which were fundamentally opposed.

Notre Jeunesse is an analysis of the growth and formation of the two bodies of thought which had split France and the French tradition from top to bottom since the Revolution, and of the process in which Tradition had been divorced from Freedom.

It is at this point in his work that Péguy first makes the distinction associated with his name, between a *mystique* and a *politique*. Both schools of thought, the democratic republican and the Catholic Royalist parties, were born of a *mystique*, a faith, and both, following the natural law of degeneration, had ended as *politiques*, sacrificing their belief in freedom to the desire for power. As *mystiques* they were opposed but not, as Belloc says, divided by any process of reason. But once they had become *politiques*, political parties, solely concerned with the triumph of their policies, they had hardened into ideologies of Left and Right. France had been "de-Christianized" in the same way and to the same extent to which the Republican party had been "derepublicanized" and to Péguy the history of France in the nineteenth century is a long process of "de-mystification," a natural tendency which always threatens a *mystique*. A substantial part of *Notre Jeunesse* consists of a survey of French history in the nineteenth century examined in the light of his theories. These are taken up and developed in the opening pages of *Clio*, with special reference to the need for Christianity always to return to its source, its *mystique,* and to *refound* its institutions by allowing the *mystique* the freedom to create tradition afresh.

Unlike Belloc, who denies the "de-Christianization" of France, Péguy therefore maintains that it was an accomplished fact. In a sense both are right, because they are speaking on entirely different levels. As a *politique,* as an institution and as an organized body, Roman Catholicism in France in 1910 was stronger and more coherent than it had ever been under the Third Republic. It had not only survived the Separation of Church and State, the abrogation of the Concordat, but had evolved a coherent and convincing body of doctrines. The anticlerical measures carried through by Combes, the Radical President of the Council, with the backing of Jaurès and the Socialists, had not only put an end to all hopes of reconciliation, they had consolidated the Right. In 1891, Leo XIII had tried to rally the Catholics to the Republic in an attempt to end the strife. But the Dreyfus Affair had produced the opposite result and turned his policy of *ralliement* upside down. The Left had gained a Pyrrhic victory and their misuse of their triumph in the Dreyfus Affair had created a strong and united Catholic Front led by Charles Maurras and the men of the *Action Française.* For the first time since the days of Lamennais, Catholicism in France had recovered its prestige in the intellectual world. It was the strength of that movement in politics, letters and scholarship, represented by the names of Maurras, Daudet, Claudel, Maritain and others, which justified Belloc in saying that the attempt to "de-Christianize" France had failed; and it was its philosophy which justified

Péguy in asserting the opposite. But it was not until 1926, when the *Action Française* was condemned by the Vatican, that Péguy's point of view was fully understood.

Notre Jeunesse deals principally with the political issues involved. In *Clio I* he turns to the religious question and in a diatribe against the clergy makes them solely responsible for the degeneration of the Catholic *mystique* into a *politique* and the failure to meet the new situation created by the Revolution. Historically, Péguy's version of the failure of Catholicism in the modern world is in certain respects false to the facts. In the first place he ignores the existence of the democratic party within the French Church, though since the nineties it had been a growing force with a large support among the lower clergy. The Bishops and the higher clergy in general had remained solidly antagonistic to any reconciliation with the Republic, even after the policy of *ralliement* had been officially proclaimed by Leo XIII. Their attitude was unchanged in 1926 at the time of the condemnation of the *Action Française*. The fact that the Catholic party took its ideas from a declared atheist, Maurras, who identified mysticism and romanticism, illustrates the extent to which the Catholic *politique* had become divorced from its *mystique*. But it is also significant for Péguy's point of view that he took no account of the *curés démocrates* and regarded them as Modernists. Liberal Catholicism was to him no less a *politique* than Conservative Catholicism. As far as I can recall, the name of Lamennais never occurs in his pages and he certainly had more respect for the "implacable, impeccable, invincible logic" of the *Action Française* than for the rhetoric of *Paroles d'un Croyant*.

Halévy's well-balanced account of Péguy's difficulties fully

describes the reasons for his isolation. Péguy was still an un-
repentant idealist and, though since 1908 a Catholic, refused
to deny *his* socialism and refused to join the Catholic party.
Péguy, Halévy writes, was never a democrat, and what is perhaps almost as misleading, suggests that he might be called a
liberal. In fact any attempt to label Péguy politically is a waste
of time, though it would be equally false to accept his own
statement that he was a *mystique* if that implies political impar-
tiality or indifference. Péguy was always deeply involved in
politics and a large proportion of his essays are political pamphlets. But his attitude is only paradoxical as long as his conception of a *mystique* is overlooked. The importance of *Clio I*
is that it makes his meaning clear beyond all argument, and
removes any obscurities which the practical purpose of *Notre
Jeunesse* may have involved. A *mystique*, he there says, is an
"operation" which links the eternal and the temporal spheres,
a movement which is the sole guarantee of freedom. His sav-
age attack on the clerics in *Clio I* is directed against their failure to fulfill their office as guardians of the Christian *mystique* and to ensure that the source of inspiration continues to
"nourish the world." Their fault consists in having misunderstood the relation between a *mystique* and a *politique*, and in
having allowed a legal and political conception of Church and
State to obscure and finally conceal the proper relations between religion and politics in the widest sense of the word. The
whole temporal life of mankind depended on a conception of
the relation between religion and culture and the State. This
had been completely forgotten during the nineteenth century,
and as a result Roman Catholicism, particularly in France,
had lost all touch with the people. That is why Péguy, at one

and the same time, attacks both forms of political Catholicism, the reactionaries of the Right and the progressives of the Left. And it was not until both forms had been in turn condemned (the *Sillon* in 1906 and the *Action Française* in 1926) that Péguy's thought began to make headway.

Since then Péguy has of course been used and appropriated by both Right and Left. But it is a testimony to his integrity that his work has inspired very divergent policies, as may be seen from the cases of Bernanos and Mounier. For although Bernanos began as a Camelot du Roi, and Mounier became the spokesman of the Left in Catholicism, their attitude is fundamentally different from the political Catholicism of the nineteenth century. Their *politiques* are the expression of the Christian *mystique* and breathe an atmosphere of freedom unknown to the Roman Catholicism of the nineteenth century. That change owes much to Péguy who rediscovered the Christian *mystique* in the "great debate" of the Dreyfus Affair.

ALEXANDER DRU

*Memories
of Youth*

A Family of Fouriérist Republicans — the Milliets

After so many lucky chances, what good fortune for our *Ca-hiers* to be able to begin today publishing the archives of a republican family. When M. Paul Milliet first came to me with his proposals, with the incurable modesty of people who really have something to offer, he did not fail to begin by apolo-gizing, saying: "You'll see. They include some of Hugo's and Béranger's letters." (Meaning to justify himself on the score that there were some *documents* among the papers he was offering, *historical* documents, on *historic* figures, unpublished of course.) "There are letters about the conquest of Algeria, about the Mexican expedition, the Crimean War. (Or perhaps, more probably, the Italian War.)" (He meant to justify himself, on the grounds that among his papers there were some *his-torical* documents about the great events of *history,* authentic naturally, and, of course, unpublished. I said: "No.")

"No, don't apologize. On the contrary, be proud of your family papers. Letters by Béranger, letters by Hugo, we've got roomfuls of them. We're up to the neck in them. The Libraries are full of them, it's what they are made of (and what they are made for). It's even what Librarians are made of. And we too, the Librarians' friends. We've enough, enough, enough. More are published every day. And when there are no more

3

left, they will go on appearing. Because if need be, we'll make more. And the family will help us to make more. Because there will always be the author's royalties to draw on."

But what we want, *what we cannot make,* are letters by people who are not Victor Hugo, Quinet, Raspail, Blanqui, Fouriér — they're all very fine. But what we want to know exactly, precisely, is what troops, what admirable troops, those thinkers, those republican leaders, those great founders of the Republic had behind them.

That is what we want to have, what nobody can forge.

History will always tell us about the big chiefs, the leaders of history, more or less well, less rather than more, that's its *métier;* and if history does not, then historians will, and if historians do not then the professors (of history) will. What we want to know, and what we cannot invent, what we want to know more about, are not the principal rôles, the leading stars, the grand drama, the stage, the spectacle; what we want to know is what went on behind, below, beneath the surface, what the people of France were like; in fact, what we want to know is the *tissue* of the people in that heroic age, the texture of the republican party. What we want to know is the texture, the very tissue of the bourgeoisie, of the Republic, of the people, when the bourgeoisie was great, when the people was great, when the republicans were heroic, and the Republic had clean hands. And to leave nothing unsaid, when Republicans were republicans, and the Republic was the republic. What we want is not a Sunday version of history, but the history of every day of the week, a people in the ordinary texture of its daily life; working and earning, working for its daily bread, *panem quotidianum;* a race in its reality, displayed in all its depth.

However, if we come across some of Hugo's letters and some verses by Béranger we shall not make a point of eliminating them. In the first place, Hugo and Béranger came from people like that. And with families like theirs one must always be on one's guard against lawsuits.

How these men lived, who were our ancestors and whom we acknowledge as our masters, how these people who liked work worked; people who were not only hard-working, but worked hard, who enjoyed work, working together as a whole, bourgeois and people, happily and healthily; who had a veritable cult for work; a cult, a religion of work well done. Of work completed. And how a whole people, a whole race, friends and enemies alike, all adversaries, and yet all friends, were bursting with sap and health and joy, that is what will be found in these archives, or to speak more modestly, in the papers of this republican family.

You will see what culture is, and how utterly different from (infinitely more precious than) science, archaeology, a doctrine, erudition, and, of course, a system. You will see what culture was like before the professors crushed it. You will see what a people was like before it was obliterated by a "primary" mentality.

You will see what culture was in the days when there was culture; how almost indefinable it is, a whole age, a whole world, of which we today no longer have any notion. You will see the marrow of our race, the cellular tissue. What a French family was like. You will see characters. All that we no longer see, all that we don't see nowadays. How the children did their studies in the days when there were studies.

In a word everything we no longer see today.

You will see, in the very tissue, what a cell was like, a family;

not one of the families that founded dynasties, the great republican dynasties; but one of the families that was, as it were,
a dynasty of the people, of the republic. A dynasty of the common tissue of the Republic.

Families which count because they belong to the common
tissue.

How a certain number, a small number, perhaps, of those
families, of those common dynasties, usually intermarrying,
weaving themselves in and out among each other like threads,
by filiation, by alliances, made and provided, not only the
whole history of the Republic, but the people of the Republic.
Those families, almost always the same ones, wove the history
of what historians would call the Republican Movement, and
that we shall resolutely call, that must be called, the procla-
mation of the republican *mystique*. The Dreyfus Affair having
been the last movement, the supreme effort of that heroism,
of that *mystique* the last manifestation, the last revelation of
those families.

Halévy is inclined to think, and I should be ready to agree
with him, that the Republic was founded, preserved and saved
and is still sustained by a small number of loyal families. Do
they still preserve it in the same way? As they did for a century or more, in a sense almost since the second half of the
eighteenth century? I am ready to agree with him, that a
small number of families, of dynastic, hereditary loyalties,
preserved the tradition, the *mystique* and what Halévy very
rightly calls "*republican conservation.*" But where I should not,
perhaps, follow him, is that I think that we are literally the
last representatives, and, unless our children take on the task,
almost the last, posthumous survivals.

In any case, the last *witnesses*.

I mean precisely this: we do not yet know whether our children will reunite the threads of tradition, of the republican *mystique*. It has become completely foreign to the intermediary generation — and that makes twenty years.

We are the rearguard; not only a rearguard, but a somewhat isolated rearguard, sometimes almost abandoned. A company left in the lurch. We are almost specimens. We are going to be, we ourselves will be, archives, tablets, fossils, witnesses and survivors from those historic times. Tablets to be consulted.

We are extremely badly placed. Chronologically. In the succession of generations. We are the rearguard, in very poor touch, out of touch with the main body, the generations of the past. We are the last generation with a republican *mystique*. And our Dreyfus Affair will have been the last operation of the republican *mystique*.

We are the last. Almost the ones after the last. Immediately after us begins the world we call, which we have called, which we shall not cease calling, the modern world. The world that tries to be clever. The world of the intelligent, of the advanced, of those who know, who don't have to be shown a thing twice, who have nothing more to learn. The world of those who are not had on by fools. Like us. *That is to say:* the world of those who believe in nothing, not even in atheism, who devote themselves, who sacrifice themselves to nothing. *More precisely:* the world of those without a *mystique*. And who boast of it. Let no one make a mistake, and no one, consequently, rejoice over it, on either side. The *derepublicani{ation* of France is essentially the same movement as the *de-Christiani{ation* of France. Both together are one and the same movement, a profound *demystification*. It is one and the same movement which makes people no longer believe in the Republic and no longer believe in God, no longer want to lead a republican life, and no longer want to lead a Christian life, they have had enough of it, and one might almost say that they no longer believe in idols, and that they no longer want to believe in idols, and that they no longer want to believe in the true God. The *same* incredulity, *one single* incredulity, strikes at the idols and at God, strikes at the false gods and the true God, the old God and the new gods, the ancient gods and the God of the Christians. One and the same sterility withers the city and Christendom. The political city and the Christian city. The city of man and the City of God. That is the specific sterility of modern times. Let no one, therefore, rejoice on seeing the misfortune that befalls his enemy, his adversary, his neighbor. For the *same* misfortune, the same sterility, falls upon him. As I have often said in these *Cahiers*, in the days when I was not read, the argument is not really between the Republic and the Monarchy, between republicanism and royalism, particularly if one considers them as political forms, as two political forms; the modern world is not only opposed to the old *régime* and the new *régime* in France, it is opposed and contrary to all old cultures, to all old *régimes*, to all old cities, to everything which is culture, to everything which is the city. In fact, it is the first time in the history of the world that a whole world lives and prospers, *appears* to prosper, *in opposition to all culture*.

But let me not be misunderstood. I don't say this will last forever. Our race has seen as bad times. But, anyway, that is how things stand.

And there we are.

We even have very deep reasons for hoping that it will not be for long.

We are extremely badly placed. We are in fact situated at a critical point, a distinguishing point, a dividing line. We are placed between the generations which had the republican *mystique* and those which have not got it, between those who still have it and those who no longer have it. So no one believes us. On either side. *Neutri,* neither the ones nor the others. The old republicans do not want to believe that there are no more young republicans. The young do not want to believe that there were old republicans.

We are between the two. No one, therefore, will believe us. To both we seem wrong. When we say to the old republicans: be careful, there's no one to come after us, they shrug their shoulders. They think there always will be someone. And when we say to the young: be careful, don't talk so airily about the Republic, it was not always a pack of politicians, behind it there is a *mystique,* it has its *mystique,* behind it lies a glorious past, an honorable past, and what is perhaps more important still, nearer the essence, there is a whole race behind it, heroism and perhaps sanctity; when we say that to the young, they stare at us with mild contempt and start treating us as old fogies.

Ready to regard us as fanatics.

But I repeat, I do not say it is forever. On the contrary, the deepest reasons, the most serious indications all make us believe, and oblige us to think that the next generation, the generation which comes immediately after the generation which comes immediately after us, and which will soon be our children's generation, is going to be a mystical generation. Our race has too much blood in its veins to remain for more than a generation in the ashes and mildew of criticism. It is too vital not to reintegrate itself, organically, at the end of a generation.

Everything leads one to think that the two *mystiques,* the republican and the Christian, will flower again at the same time. As part of the same movement. In a single movement, just as they disappeared together (momentarily), and as they were obliterated together. However, what I say goes for the present, for the whole present. And after all much may happen in the course of a generation.

Misfortunes may befall us.

Such is our meager position. We are meager. As thin as a blade. We are squeezed in and flattened between the antecedent generations on the one hand, and on the other hand an already thick layer of succeeding generations. Such is the principal reason for our meagerness, our thinness, the wretchedness of our situation. We have the ungrateful task, the meager office, the meager duty of keeping the communications between them open, of enlightening the ones about the others, of informing them about one another. We shall, therefore, as a rule, be spewed out by the one and the other. That is commonly the fate of anyone who tries to tell a little (of the) truth.

We are charged, as though by chance, with making people communicate through us who do not want to communicate. Charged with informing people who have no wish to be informed.

I am horrified when I see, when I discover, that the older men among us do not want to see what is self-evident, and which only has to be seen to be believed: the extent to which the young have become estranged from everything related to republican thought and its *mystique*. This is seen, above all, naturally, in the fact that thoughts, which were thoughts to us, have become, for them, ideas, in the fact that what was to us an instinct, a race, thoughts, have become for them *propositions*, from the fact that what was to us organic, has become for them a matter of logic.

Thoughts, instinct, races, habits which were nature itself to us, which we took for granted, on which we lived, and which were the forms of life, and which consequently no one thought about, which were more than legitimate, more than unquestioned: unreasoned, have become what is worst of all: theses, historical theses, hypotheses, I mean all that is least solid, most inexistent. The basis of a thesis. When a *régime*, from being organic has become logical, and from being alive has become historical, that *régime* is done for.

Today we prove and demonstrate the Republic. When it was alive no one proved it.

One lived it. When a *régime* is demonstrated, easily, comfortably, victoriously, that means it is hollow, done for.

The Republic today is a thesis, accepted by the young. Accepted, rejected; it doesn't matter which. Proved, refuted. What is important, what is serious, what signifies, is not that it is held up, bolstered up, more or less indifferently, but that it should be a thesis.

That means that it *must* be supported or held together.

When a *régime* is a thesis among others (among so many others) it is down and out. A *régime* which is standing, which is alive, is not a thesis.

"What does it matter?" say the professionals, the politicians. "What does it matter to us? What can it matter to us? We have excellent administrators. So what can it matter to us? It works well. We are not, it is true, republicans any longer, but we do know how to govern. Indeed we know how to govern far better than when we were republicans," they say. "Or rather when we were republicans we had no idea at all how to govern. And now," they modestly add, "now we are beginning to know, just a little. Look at the elections. They are good. They are always good. And they will be better still. All the better because it is we who make them. And because we are beginning to know how to make them. The Right lost a million votes. We could just as easily have made them lose fifty and a half million. But we are moderate. The Government makes the elections; the elections make the Government. You get your money back. The government makes the electors, and the electors make the government. The government makes the Deputies. The Deputies make the government. The country pays. And every one consents. It is not a vicious circle as you might suppose. It is not at all vicious. It is a circle, and nothing more, a perfect circle, a closed circle. All circles are closed. Otherwise they would not be circles. It is not precisely what our founders foresaw. But our founders did not manage all that well. And then one cannot go on founding indefinitely.[1] It would be tiring. The proof that it is lasting, that it stands up to it, is that it has gone on for forty years. There is no reason why it should not go on for "forty centuries." The first forty years are the worst. It's the first forty years that count. After-

---

1. *Cf.* the opening theme of *Clio I*.

wards, one gets used to it. A country, a *régime* does not need you, it does not need mystics, a *mystique*, or its *mystique*. That would only embarrass it. For such a long journey. It needs a sound *politique*, which means a good government policy."

They are mistaken. The politicians are mistaken. From the summit of the Republic forty centuries (of the future) do not look down upon them. If the republic has worked for the last forty years, it is because everything has worked for the last forty years. If the republic is solid in France, it is not because the republic is solid in France, it's because everything is solid everywhere. In modern history, though not in all history, there are great waves of crises, usually going out from France (1789–1815, 1830, 1848), which shake everything from one end of the world to the other. And then there are longer or shorter periods of calm, periods of flat calm which pacify everything for a shorter or longer time. There are *epochs* and there are *periods*. We are in a period. If the republic has settled down it is not because it is the republic (this Republic), and not through any merit of its own, but because it is, because we are, in a period. The duration of the Republic no more proves the lasting quality of the Republic than the duration of the neighboring Monarchies proves the lasting quality of Monarchy. They belong to the same age. That is all it proves.

When the republicans argue from the fact that the republic endures in order to prove the proposition that it is lasting, they seem to be proving what is self-evident. And yet they are begging the question, are guilty of a *petitio principi*. For what is lasting in the republic is *la durée*, duration. It is not the *régime* which is lasting, but time. The tranquillity of a certain period of history.

But when the reactionaries, on the other hand, the monarchists, show us and demonstrate with their usual complacency, equal and contrary to that of the others, and use the duration of the neighboring monarchies as an argument, their solidity and tranquillity (and even, in a certain sense their prosperity, though here in a sense they are on firmer ground), they are following, in their own way, not only exactly the same sort of reasoning, but the same reasoning. They are committing the same anticipation, a contrary anticipation, and the same distortion. The republicans and the monarchists, the governing republicans and the royalist theoreticians, reason in the same way, because they are intellectuals both together and separately, together and contrary to one another; they are politicians, and believe in a certain sense in politics, speak a political language, move and are situated on a political plane. So they speak the same language and move on the same plane. They believe in *régimes*, and that it is the *régime* which makes peace and war, provides the strength and virtue, the health and sickness, the steadiness, the duration and the tranquillity of a people. The strength of a race. It is as though one believed that the Châteaux of the Loire caused or did not cause earthquakes.

We believe on the contrary (in opposition to both sides) that there are infinitely deeper forces and realities, and that it is the people on the contrary who are the strength or the weakness of *régimes;* and much less *régimes* of the people.

We believe that neither side sees nor wants to see those forces, those infinitely deeper realities.

If the republic and the neighboring monarchies enjoy the same tranquillity, it is because they are bathed in the same period, walking together along the same corridor. It is because they lead the same life fundamentally, are following the same diet. On those matters the republicans and the monarchists reason conjointly, though in opposition. We, on the other hand, place ourselves on an entirely different plane, descending on to a different level; trying to descend to quite other depths, we think, we believe, on the contrary, that it is the people who make the *régimes*, peace and war, strength and weakness, sickness and health.

We therefore turn toward the young, we turn to another side, and we can only say: "Take care. You treat us as old fogies. That's quite all right. But take care. When you talk airily, when you treat the Republic lightly, you do not only risk being unjust (which is not perhaps very important, at least so you say, in your system, but risk what in your system *is* serious), you risk something much worse, you risk being stupid. You forget, you fail to recognize that there is a republican *mystique;* but ignoring it and failing to recognize it will not prevent its having existed. Men have died for liberty as men have died for the Faith. The elections, nowadays, seem to you a grotesque formality, uniformly false and bogus in every respect. You have the right to say so. But men have lived, men without number, heroes, martyrs and I would even say saints—and when I say *saints* perhaps I know what I am saying—

men have lived, numberless men, heroically, like saints, and have suffered and died, a whole people lived in order that the last of fools today should have the right to accomplish that bogus formality. It was a laborious and fearful birth. It was not always grotesquely funny. And all around us other peoples, whole races, are laboring in the same agonizing birth, working and struggling for that contemptible formality. The elections nowadays are ridiculous. But there was a time, my dear Variot, a heroic time, when the sick and the dying had themselves carried on their chairs in order *to deposit their ballot in the urn*. To deposit one's ballot in the urn; to you, today, the expression is pure comedy. It was prepared by a century of heroism. Not by literary heroism, that costs nothing. But by a century of incontestable heroism, of the most authentic quality. And, I should add, typically French. The elections are ridiculous. But there was an election. The great divide in the world, the great election of the modern world, between the *ancien régime* and the Revolution. And what a ballot it was, Jean Variot. There was that little ballot which began by the mill of Valmy, and that barely ended on the heights of Hougoumont. Moreover, it ended, like all political affairs, in a sort of clumsy compromise, between the two parties present.

"The elections are ridiculous. But the heroism and the holiness with which one obtains contemptible results, temporally contemptible, are the greatest and most sacred things in the world. The most beautiful. You reproach us with the temporal degradation of the results. Look at yourselves. Look at your own results. You are always talking about republican degradation. But isn't the degradation of a *mystique* into a *politique* the common law? You talk of the decay of the republic, that is to say of the collapse of the republican *mystique* into a republican *politique*. Have there not been, are there not other degradations? Everything begins as a *mystique* and ends as a *politique*. Everything begins with *la mystique*, in mysticism, with its own *mystique*, and everything ends in politics, in *la politique*, in a policy. The important point is not that such and such a *politique* should triumph over another such, and that one should succeed. The whole point (what matters), the essential thing, is that *in each order, in each system,* THE MYSTIQUE SHOULD NOT BE DEVOURED BY THE POLITIQUE TO WHICH IT GAVE BIRTH.

"The essential thing, the thing that matters, is not that such and such a policy should triumph, but that in each order, in each system, in each *mystique,* the *mystique* should not be devoured by the policy that issues from it.

"In other words, it possibly matters, it obviously does matter, that the republicans should carry the day against the royalists, or that the royalists should carry the day against the republicans, but that is of infinitely little importance compared with the importance of the republicans remaining republicans.

"And I would add, not merely for the sake of symmetry, I should add as complementary: that the royalists should be and remain royalists. Which is, perhaps, what they are not doing at the present moment, just when they think they are doing so. You are always talking to us of the degradation of republicanism. But has there not been, by virtue of the same movement, has there not been a parallel degradation of monarchism, a similar royalist degradation? This is to say, properly speaking, a degradation of the royalist *mystique* into a certain policy issuing from it and corresponding to it, into a royalist policy. Have we not seen the effects of that *politique* for centuries, do we not see them daily? Have we not for centuries watched the royalist *mystique* being devoured by the royalist *politique?* And even today, although the royalist party is not in power, do we not read daily in its two principal newspapers, do we not see the miserable effects of that policy daily; and I should even go so far as to say that for those who know how to read, a constant struggle, a continual tension, an almost painful struggle, really painful, between a *mystique* and a *politique*, between their *mystique* and their *politique*, the *mystique* belonging of course to the *Action Française*, using a rationalist terminology which deceives none but themselves; the *politique* being that of the *Gaulois* using a worldly terminology. What would they be like if they were in power? (Like us, alas.)"

People are always talking of the degradation of republicanism. When one sees what the clerical *politique* has made of the Christian *mystique*, why be astonished at what the radical policy has made of the republican *mystique?* When one sees what the clerks have, in general, made of the saints, why be surprised at what our parliamentarians have made of heroes? When one sees what the reactionaries have, by and large, made of sanctity, why be astonished at what the revolutionaries have made of heroism?

And then, all the same, one must be fair. If one wants to compare one order with another, one system with another, one must compare them on the same plane. One must compare the *mystiques* with one another and the *politiques* with one another. One must not compare a *mystique* with a *politique;*

nor a *politique* with a *mystique*. In all the primary schools of the Republic, and in some of the secondary schools, and in many of the high schools they never tire of comparing the royalist *politique* and the republican *mystique*. In the *Action Française* everything comes down to comparing the republican *politique* with the royalist *mystique*. There is no end to it.

No one will ever agree. But that is perhaps what the parties want.

Perhaps it is the party game.

Our masters in the primary schools once used to hide the *mystique* of the *ancien régime* from us, the *mystique* of the old France, and concealed ten centuries of France from us. Today our adversaries want to conceal *the mystique of the old France which was the republican mystique.*

And in particular the revolutionary mystique.

For the quarrel is not, as is said, between the old *régime* and the Revolution. The old *régime* was a *régime* belonging to the old France. The Revolution is eminently the work, the operation of the old France. The dividing date is not the first of January 1789 between midnight and one minute after midnight. The dividing line is somewhere about 1881.

Here again the republicans and the royalists, the republican government and the royalist theoreticians, reason in the same way, give two complementary arguments, twin arguments. Our good masters at the primary school told us, in effect, that, up to the first of January 1789 (Paris time), our poor old France was an abyss of darkness and ignorance, of horrifying miseries, of crude barbarity (in fact, they did their job, taught their lesson), and so well you could hardly believe it: on the first of January 1789, electric light was installed everywhere. Our good adversaries in the School opposite told us, roughly speaking, that up to the first of January 1789, nature's sun was shining; since the first of January 1789, we have only got electric light. Both the ones and the others exaggerate.

The argument is not between an *ancien régime,* an old France, that supposedly ended in 1789, and a new France supposedly beginning in 1789. The fight goes much deeper. It is between the whole of the old France, pagan France (the Renaissance, the humanities, culture, ancient and modern letters, Greek and Latin and French), Christian France, traditional and revolutionary, monarchist, royalist and republican — and on the other hand, on the other side, in opposition, the dominion of a certain form of elementary, primary thought, which became established about 1881, which is not the Republic though calling itself the Republic, which is a parasite on the Republic and is properly speaking the domination of the intellectual party.

The contest is not between heroes and saints; the fight is against the intellectuals, against those who despise heroes and saints equally.

The argument is not between two orders of greatness. The fight is between those who hate greatness itself, who hate the one and the other equally, who have made themselves the official upholders of all that is base, small-minded and vile.

That is what bursts out with striking evidence in the papers of this republican Fouriérist family, or rather, for it is not quite as compact as that, in the *Cahiers,* the notebooks of that repub-

lican family. And good heavens, if there are some of Hugo's
letters among them — well, we will publish them. We shall not
be unkind. We shall do nothing to harm that great memory.
But we shall publish above all the files, the papers, of the Milliets. And it will be seen that the very tissue of the republican
party was heroic, and what is almost more important, how
cultivated it was; how classical; in a word, for anyone who
knows how to read, how deeply rooted in the old France, and
at bottom, in the *ancien régime*.

Our collaborator M. Daniel Halévy has pointed out in these
very *Cahiers*, and emphasized very clearly and very well that
the history of the last century is not all of a piece: it is not as
simple as it looks, is not a single block, does not run along a
single track, in a single direction. It is not simple, univocal,
unilateral. There never has been such a thing as an *ancien
régime* which lasted for centuries, followed, one fine day, by
a revolution to overthrow the *ancien régime;* followed by an
offensive from the *ancien régime* and its return to power; and
then a struggle, a debate, a contest between *ancien régime* and
revolution, lasting a century. The reality is much less simple.
Halévy showed quite clearly that the Republic too had a tradition, a principle of conservation (the Republic above all,
perhaps), and that the Republic in particular had a tradition of
conservatism. The difference, the distance between the two
hypotheses emerges, and is seen above all, naturally, at certain critical moments: for example, in the *coups d'état*. According to the first hypothesis, the first theory, the theory
of the single bloc, the rigid theory, the two *coups* were both
movements of the same order, moving in the same direction,

of the same tenor and mold. The same movement twice repeated. The 2nd December, 1852, is a repetition of the 18 Brumaire, which in its turn is a first edition of the 2nd December. That is what is taught as a sort of twin teaching, both by the State Schoolmasters and by the reactionaries. To the schoolmasters, the teachers (and to Victor Hugo in particular), the two *coups d'état* are two crimes, the same crime repeated. To the reactionaries the two *coups d'état* are police operations, twin actions by the police, both successful, recommencing one another.

A single movement at two different times. Brumaire and December. That is the double idea of Hugo and the Bonapartists.

The reality is very much less simple, very much more complex and perhaps even very much more complicated. The French Revolution founded a tradition that had already been prepared for a number of years, it founded a new order, a new conservatism. And a number of intelligent men have been led to think, nowadays, that the new order is not worth the old. But it certainly founded a new order, and not a disorder, as the reactionaries maintain. That order degenerated and became disorder, followed by disorders which became serious under the Directoire.

Now, if, as we must, we call Restorations restorations of a certain order, of one or the other type, and if we call the introduction of disorder(s) *disturbances, perturbations,* the 18 Brumaire[2] certainly came as a restoration (both republican and monarchist inseparably, which confers on it quite a particular

2. The French custom of referring to days rather than to years, necessitated by the number of crises, is so confusing that I append a list of the events which Péguy

interest, and gives it its own tone, a special meaning, making it, really, a very singular operation, comparable to nothing else, that deserves close study, and to which, above all, one should compare nothing in the whole of the nineteenth century in France, or even in the whole of French history, to which in fact no other French operation can be compared, to which there is no analogy except possibly in the history of other countries); (above all, one must be on one's guard against comparing it to the 2nd December;) 1830 was a republican restoration; but I was forgetting, one always forgets, Louis XVIII; the Restoration was a monarchical restoration; 1830 a republican restoration; 1848 a restoration (republican); the days of

---

seems to be referring to. The "days of May" I take to be a reference to the 16th May and not the 28th of the same month.

18 *Brumaire*.	9th November, 1799. The overthrow of the Directoire and revision of the Constitution. Bonaparte First Consul.
2nd December.	1851. The *coup d'état*, by which Louis Napoleon established his power, altered the Constitution in preparation for the Second Empire.
1830.	The abdication of Charles X. Louis Philippe raised to the throne by the Assembly.
1848.	Flight of Louis Philippe (February 22). Beginning of the Second Republic.
Days of June.	1848, renewed outbreak of the "revolution" held in check by the conservatives and put down by Larominière.
4th September.	1870. Proclamation of the Third Republic.
31st October.	Another "*journée*," and a foretaste of the Commune.
18th March.	Outbreak of the Commune. The Government under Thiers at Versailles.
Days of May.	MacMahon's attempt to use the President's right to dissolve the Chamber in an attempt to check the Left. Considered by the Left as unconstitutional; by the Right as legitimate.
1881.	A date invented by Péguy for the beginning of the "modern world." Roughly speaking, the end of the Conservative Republic and the beginning of the era of scandals: Boulanger, *Affaire* Wilson, Panama Scandal, Dreyfus Affair.

June were an explosion, a second, redoubled explosion of the republican *mystique;* the 2nd December, on the contrary, was a *disturbance,* an introduction of disorder, the gravest disorder (disturbance) perhaps in the history of the nineteenth century in France; it introduced, and brought into the world not only into the head, but into the body itself, into the nation and the tissue of the body politic, and the social body, a new personnel, a purely political, demagogic personnel, untouched by any *mystique;* it was really the introduction of demagogy; the 4th September was a restoration (republican); the 31st October and the 22nd January, even, a republican day; the 10th March, even, was a republican restoration in a certain sense, and not just a heightening of the temperature, a sudden volcanic fever, but rather a second revolt, a second explosion of the republican and nationalist *mystique;* the days of May were certainly a disturbance and not a restoration; the Republic was a restoration until about 1881 when the intrusion of the tyranny of the intellectuals and the domination of the primary mind began to make it a government of disorder.

In that sense, and that sense only, the 2nd December was a punishment (*le Châtiment, l'Expiation,* in Hugo's words) for the 18th Brumaire, and the Second Empire was the punishment for the First. But far from being the answer to the first, the Second Empire was in a sense everything that was most contrary to the first. The First Empire was a *régime* of order, of a certain order. It was even, in spite of a lot of indiscipline, and military indiscipline even, a sort of apotheosis of discipline, an eminently military discipline. It was a *régime* great in order and great in history. The Second Empire was a *régime* of disorder(s) of every kind. It really introduced disorder, a certain disorder, and installed a certain group, a certain clique and class, very *modern*, very *advanced*, respected by no one, not at all *ancienne France*, not in the least *ancien régime*. Or again one might say that the Second Empire was the coarsest form of "*Boulangisme*" [3] we have had, and moreover, the only form that succeeded.

The Revolution, on the contrary, the great Revolution, had been an inauguration. A more or less fortunate inauguration, but, in any case, an inauguration.

An inauguration; that is to say, that every subsequent restoration was nothing more than a repetition, a pale image, an attempted renewal of that inauguration.

In other words the First Empire was not what we call Caesarism. The Second Empire [4] was what we call Caesarism. And *Boulangisme* was Caesarism. There was a lot of Caesarism among the anti-Dreyfusists. There was none in Dreyfusism. The Combist [5] domination was genuine Caesarism. The

3. *Boulangisme*. General Georges Boulanger (1837–1891) was a farcical figure thrown up by the general feeling of distrust in the Constitution which he promised to "revise." He was the creature of Clémenceau who urged his appointment as Minister of War. He stood for election and soon obtained almost as many votes as Louis Napoleon. The Left who thought to use him were soon disappointed. "Boulboul," as Clémenceau called him, by the use of ingenious accommodations was subsidized by the Right to the tune of three millions. He was not a success in the Chamber and his attempt to dominate it failed lamentably. "*Monsieur, à votre âge, Bonaparte était mort,*" evoked no reply from him. The Royalists were implicated in his policy of "revision."

4. Péguy writes *deuxième* instead of *seconde* Empire, to deflate it.

5. *Combisme*. Combes (Émile), born in 1835, Président du Conseil on the retirement of Waldeck-Rousseau, the sea-green incorruptible of anticlericalism. A former seminary student, he voted the Separation of Church and State and the anticlerical

most dangerous of all, because it was one that masqueraded
as republicanism. The domination of the Radicals and the
Radical-Socialists is properly speaking Caesarism, the multi-
Caesarism of electoral committees.

One must be very careful not to judge by names and indeed appearance, and one must mistrust them so much that
just as the Second Empire, historically and really, is not the
continuation of the First Empire, so the Third Republic, really
and historically, does not *continue* itself. The continuation of
the Third Republic does not *continue* the beginning of the
Third Republic. Without there having been any great event,
I mean any inscribable historical event, in 1881, the Republic then began to reveal its discontinuity. From having been a
republic it became Caesarism.

Not only can one say: everything is explained, I would say,
everything is illuminated by that distinction. The incredible
difficulties of public and private action are suddenly illuminated by the full light of day, flooded in light, if only one
gives heed, gives audience so to say, to that distinction, to the
discrimination we have just recognized. The source of all the
sophism, of all the paralogisms of action, of all the *paraprag-
matisms* — or, at any rate, of all the worthwhile ones, the only
ones into which *we* can fall, the only ones we could commit,
the only innocent ones — for all their culpability — lies in the
fact that in politics we unduly prolong a line of action duly
begun as a *mystique*. A line of action had emerged and sprung

laws. Measures which did not advance the struggle against the Church in France did
not interest him. He was the embodiment of Gambetta's words: "*le cléricalisme, voilà
l'ennemi.*" A Radical, he was kept in power from 1902–1905 by the support of Jaurès
and the Socialists. This was, to Péguy, the great betrayal of Socialism.

out of a *mystique*, with its source and spring in a *mystique*.
That action was well and truly aligned. It was not only natural, legitimate, but due. Life follows its course. Action follows
action in its train. One looks through the door. There is an
engine-driver in control. Why bother about the driving? Life
carries on. Action continues. And because it continues and the
people, the mechanism, the institutions and surroundings, the
apparatus, furniture and habits, all remain the same, one fails
to notice that one has passed over the points where the line
branches off. History itself has moved forward; events themselves march on. The points have been crossed. And by the
mere succession of events, the continuation of the game, the
baseness of man and his sinfulness, the *mystique* has become
political action, or rather politics have usurped the place of the
mystique, have devoured the *mystique*. That is the unchang-
ing story that recurs again and again, only to begin all over
again. The very same action which was legitimate becomes
illegitimate. And that is how one becomes a criminal in all
innocence.

The action that was decent becomes dirty, becomes another
action, a dirty one. That is how one becomes an innocent
criminal, the most dangerous of all, perhaps.

An action begun as a *mystique* continues in politics, and
we do not notice that we are crossing the dividing line. Politics devour the *mystique*, and we fail to jump out when we are
passing over the points, the point of discrimination.

If a man with his heart in the right place discerns the dividing point, stops at that point, and refuses to move in order
to remain faithful to a *mystique*, refuses to adopt the abuses
of the political game, which is itself an abuse, and refuses to

enter into the derivative, parasitical, devouring *politique*, then politicians call him by a little word much used nowadays: they are quick to call us traitors.

Moreover, they call us traitors without conviction and for the sake of the electors. One must, after all, put something into electoral manifestos and pamphlets.

Everyone may as well know it, that is the sort of traitor we have always been and always will be. That is what we were, especially, preeminently, in the Dreyfus Affair, and the matter of Dreyfusism. The real traitor, in the full sense of the word, in the strong sense of the word, is the man who sells his faith, who sells his soul and gives himself up, *loses* his soul, betrays his principles, his ideal, his very being, who betrays his *mystique* and enters into its corresponding *politique*, the policy issuing from it and complacently passes over the dividing point.

I am not the only one. Those who subscribe to these *Cahiers* are, even now, after twelve years of deaths and new subscribers, more than two-thirds old Dreyfusards, new Dreyfusards, perpetual and impenitent Dreyfusards, mystical Dreyfusards, men of heart, little men for the most part, generally obscure, poor, and some of them very poor, who have sacrificed their careers twice, their futures, their existence, their bread: first of all to fight against their enemies, and a second time to fight against their friends; and how much more difficult that is; once to resist the politics of their enemies, and a second time to resist the policy of their friends; once in order not to succumb to their enemies and a second time so as not to succumb to their friends.

That is the sort of traitor we claim to be.

We all know what it costs. And that is why we shall always exact from our friends that respect which our enemies have never refused us.

If our first rule of conduct is not to continue (across the dividing point) an action begun as *mystique* and which ends in politics, similarly, our first rule of knowledge, of judgment, will be not to continue blindly (past the dividing point), the judgment, the knowledge, the knowing, concerned with an action begun as a *mystique* and ending in politics. Above all, one must be suspicious of one's judgment, of one's *knowing*, one's knowledge.

Above all, one must be careful of continuing. Continuing, persevering, in that sense, is all that is most dangerous to justice and to intelligence itself. To take one's ticket on departure in a party, in a faction, and never to bother where the train is rolling to, and above all, what it is rolling on, is to put oneself resolutely in the very best situation for becoming a criminal.

A great deal of light would be shed on all the rubbish, on the chatter and the nonsense and the apparent contradictions, on the difficulties and incomprehensibilities, the impossibilities, and the tiresome and tiring repetitions of the same incoherent views, on the good and bad faith of opponents — if only people would attend to what they are saying, if they made sure of talking about a *mystique* or about a *politique*. If only they would talk of the *mystique* or, more generally, of the *politique* of any particular action or order of things. That explains why, in so many polemics, and debates, the adversaries, the enemies, both seem to be in the right, and equally wrong. One of the main causes is that the one is talking about the *mys-*

tique, and the other about the *politique* issued from it. Not only justice, in the moral order, requires that one should compare two actions on the same plane, and not on different planes, the *mystique* to a *mystique* and the *politique* to a *politique;* justice in the intellectual order requires as much.

The first consequence of the distinction, a first application of that principle, is that *mystiques* are far less inimical to each other than *politiques,* and in quite a different way. *Mystiques* should not, therefore, be blamed for the faults, the wars, the dissensions, the political enmities of the *politiques. Mystiques* are much less antagonistic to one another than are *politiques.* Because unlike *politiques,* they do not invariably have to divide the temporal world, temporal matters, limited temporal power, between themselves. And when they are enemies, it is in quite a different way, at a much deeper, more essential level, and with an infinitely nobler profundity. For example, the civic *mystique,* the *mystique* of antiquity, of the city, of the suppliants, was never opposed to, never could have opposed the *mystique* of salvation in the same way that the pagan *politique* opposed the Christian *politique;* so crudely, so basely, so temporally, so morally, as the pagan Emperors opposed the Christian Emperors and vice versa. And the *mystique* of salvation can never oppose the *mystique* of liberty in the same way as the clerical *politique* opposes, for example, the Radical *politique.* It is simple enough to be a good Christian and a good citizen as long as one does not go in for politics.

When politicians exchange their *mystique* for a *politique,* they accuse you of changing if you do not follow them. Let us put it more simply, and less harshly to the great men. Their *politique* has become a merry-go-round. "Monsieur," they say, "you have changed, you are no longer at the same place. The proof is that you are no longer opposite the same horse." "*Pardon, Monsieur le Député*, it is the horses that have moved."

We have had an eminent example of this in the Dreyfus Affair, continued in the affair of Dreyfusism. One could say that where there are already so many natural difficulties, the politicians have introduced supplementary, supererogatory, artificial difficulties. They always want those who serve the *mystique* to become the agents of their *politique*, from political motives, or, more usually, from natural incomprehension. They introduce further gratuitous breaches, as though the mystical ones were not enough.

And so we have in the Dreyfus Affair a unique example, a model almost, of what is meant by the degradation of a human action; but not only that, a précis of the degradation of a *mystique* into a *politique*.

There was a singular virtue in the Affair, perhaps an eternal virtue. I mean a singular power. And we can see this clearly today now that it is all over. It was not an illusion of our youth. First of all, it should be noted that it possessed a very singular virtue. In two senses. A singular power of virtue, as long as it remained a *mystique*. A singular power of malice as soon as it entered the field of politics. One of the greatest mysteries of history and of reality, and naturally therefore one that is most easily overlooked, is the sort of absolute difference (irrevocable, irreversible), which there is in the *price* of events. The fact that certain events have a certain price, their own price; and that other events, of the same order, and of the same material or similar material, with the same form and the same value, should nevertheless have a price and value infinitely different; that every event should have its own price, its own mysterious power and value; that there should be wars and treaties of peace with their own value, heroisms and sanctities with their own value, is assuredly one of the great mysteries; that there should not only be men (and gods) who count for more than others, but peoples; entire peoples marked out in history, for the whole of temporal history, and perhaps, no doubt, for the other history too; and that the rest, the immense majority of people, almost all of them, on the contrary, should be marked out for silence, destined to silence, only rising to fall — that is a mystery we hardly see, like all great mysteries we do not observe, because we are bathed in it, as in all great mysteries; certainly it is one of the most poignant mysteries of history. The great problem of creation.

One should therefore say, with all due solemnity, that the Dreyfus Affair is one of the "chosen" events of history. It was a crisis in three histories, each of them outstanding. It was a crisis in the history of Israel. A crisis, obviously, in the history of France. And above all, it was a supreme crisis, as appears more and more distinctly, in the history of Christianity. And perhaps in several others. And thus, by a unique election, it was a triple crisis. Of triple eminence. A culmination. As for me, if I am able to continue the studies which we have begun on the situation accorded to history and to sociology in the general philosophy of the modern world,[6] following the method we always observe, of never writing anything except

6. *De la Situation Faite à l'Histoire* — three *Cahiers* published in 1907 and 1908.

what we have experienced ourselves, we shall certainly take that great crisis as an example of what a crisis is, an event with its own, eminent, price.

As for me, if I finish an infinitely more serious work and reach the age of *confessions,* which as everyone knows is at fifty years old and at nine o'clock in the morning, that is what I should most certainly propose to describe. Taking up again and concluding my old study of "the decomposition of Dreyfusism in France," I should try to give, not so much an idea, as a picture of that immortal Affair and of what it was like in reality. It was like all self-respecting affairs, essentially mystical. It lived by its *mystique.* It died of its *politique.* Such is the rule; such is the law. Such is the level of life. All parties live by their *mystique* and die by their *politique.* That is what I should try to depict. I admit I am beginning to think that it would not be entirely useless. I suspect that there are any number of misunderstandings about the Affair. And I must confess that I cannot recognize myself at all in the *portrait* Halévy traced of the Dreyfusist in these very pages.[7] I don't in the least feel like a whipped cur. I will agree to being victor; and I will agree (and this is my opinion) to having been vanquished (it all depends upon one's point of view). I don't admit for a moment to having been beaten. I admit to having been ruined (in the temporal, and greatly endangered in the eternal, order); I agree to having been deceived, and to having been fooled. I do not admit I was a wash-out. I don't in the least feel like a drowned rat. I do not recognize myself in that portrait. We were on the contrary proud, carrying our heads high, filled to

7. In the *Apology for Our Past* referred to in the Introduction.

overflowing with *military* virtue. We had, and we preserved, a very different tone, another air; we carried our heads differently, and we spoke, openly and of very different things. My mood is not at all penitential. I loathe a penitence which is not Christian, a sort of civic, lay penitence, a penitence laicized, secularized, temporalized, an imitation, a counterfeit, of penitence — a "disaffected" penitence.[8] I loathe the humiliation, the humility that is not Christian, humility but a sort of civil, civic humility, a mock humility. In civil and civic matters, in the lay or profane sphere, I prefer to be stiff with pride. And so we were. With every right. We not only had nothing to regret. There was nothing, we had done nothing that we could not pride ourselves upon.

You can begin publishing my Complete Works tomorrow morning, and even my complete words, and there is nothing in all my *Cahiers,* not a word, I would change, except for four or five words which I remember well, seven or eight words of theology, which give grounds for misunderstanding, which might be misconstrued, being in the indirect form. Not only have we nothing to disavow, there is nothing we cannot be proud of. For even in our most heated polemics, in our invective, in our pamphlets, we never failed in respect for respect. In the *Confessions of a Dreyfusist,* which will form an important part of our Confessions, there will be, as I have promised, several *Cahiers* called *Mémoires d'un Âne,* or perhaps more simply still, the *Memoirs of a Fool.* There will be none called *Memoirs of a Coward* (we will leave those to M. Jaurès, and assuredly they will not be badly done). There will be none called

8. The reference is to the Churches "disaffected to the cult" since the Combes laws.

the *Memoirs of a Turncoat; of a Penitent*. There will be none
called the *Memoirs of a Politician*. At bottom they will all be
the memoirs of a mystic.

Halévy certainly knows that I should not recognize myself.
He says so more than once, explicitly. But I am not sure that
his reader will always realize it.

Our collaborator has made it quite clear, throughout the
Cahier; he is not really dealing with us. What he wanted to do,
and what he has succeeded perfectly in giving us, is a history
of Dreyfusism; not the history or the portrait of a Dreyfusist;
or, I think his idea was the portrait or history of the average
Dreyfusist; or more exactly of a Dreyfusist in the Dreyfusist
party. But I think there is an abyss between the history and
portrait of a Dreyfusist who was in the party, and the portrait of a Dreyfusist who was not in the party. And as I read
the *Cahier* in proof, I saw the misunderstanding coming, the
double meaning, the confusion in bud. That is why I felt a
dumb revolt, dumb, of course, because I am not eloquent. I
mumbled, grumbled, stumbled, over the words as I read my
proofs, and the finer I found, the more I admired the *Cahier*,
the more I rebelled. Because the more I thought it would be
listened to. The further I thought it would carry. That is why
I want to take our collaborator to task about the proportion,
about the number of Dreyfusists his *Cahier* covers and the
number it does not cover. Those it fits and those it does not fit.
He makes certain reservations himself, draws a distinction between those who did not take part in the political demagogy,
and in particular the Combist demagogy. But where I quarrel
with him is when he seems to admit that we do not repre-

sent Dreyfusism, and that the others do represent it; when he classes us apart, as exceptions, and when all his attention is turned on the others, on those whom we are justified in calling the *politicians*. We, on the contrary, claim that we, the mystics, are and have been the heart and soul of Dreyfusism, and that we alone represent it.

Halévy sometimes seems to imply that the others followed a legitimate course or curve, and that we were wild men, almost cranks, and that it was we who made a break, a rupture, an illegitimate leap. That it is the others who were in line, and we who were out of the true. That the others are the rule, the ordinary natural run of things, and we who are not only extraordinary, but the exception, and above all, an artificial exception. People always take weakness for granted, for the rule, the normal, the usual thing. That is precisely what I contest at every level, in all degrees, at any rate, where the French race is concerned. In France, courage and honesty can perfectly well be taken for granted.

Appearances no doubt are on Halévy's side; those who appear are on his side. What I mean is that if one only considers the Dreyfusists who are to the fore, in the public eye, the journalists, publicists, lecturers, candidates, parliamentarians and politicians, all those who talk and chatter and scribble and publish, the immense majority who appear on the scene, almost the whole lot hurried to take part in the Dreyfusist demagogy, and by that I mean the political demagogy that issued from the Dreyfusist *mystique*. But what I contest is that those who *appear* in history (and whom history seizes upon, in return, with such avidity) have a great importance in the depths of reality. At that depth, where the only important realities are found, I maintain that *all* the mystical Dreyfusists remained Dreyfusists, that they remained mystics, and kept their hands clean. What does it matter whether appearances, *phenomena,* whether all the officials, all those out for profit, should have abandoned, denied, betrayed and ridiculed the *mystique* in favor of the *politique,* and of the policies which issued from it, and of political demagogy? *That,* my dear Halévy, as you yourself would say, *is life.* What does it matter if they sneer at us? We alone represent something, and they do not. What does it matter if they turn us to ridicule? They themselves live through us, and only exist by virtue of our existence. Their very vanity would not exist but for us.

And I not only claim that the mystical Dreyfusists remained Dreyfusists and mystics. I contend that they are the greater number, and remained the greater number. Even in the crude sense, and not just as quality, as virtue, but quantitatively; it is they who counted and they who count.

Mysticism may be the laughing stock of politics, but all the same, it is the mystic who nourishes politics.

For the politically minded always recover their balance, and think they can save themselves, by saying that they at least are practical, and that we are not. That is precisely where they are mistaken. Where they mislead. We do not even grant them that. It is the mystic who is practical, and the politically minded who are not. It is we who are practical, *who do something,* and it is they who are not, *who do nothing.* It is we who accumulate and they who squander. It is we who build, lay foundations, and it is they who demolish. It is we who nourish, and they who are the parasites. It is we who make things and men, peoples and races. It is they who wreak ruin.

The little which they are, they are by virtue of us. Their very misery, vanity, emptiness, infirmity, frivolity, vileness, the nothing which they are, is only theirs by virtue of us.

That is why there can be no question of their inspecting us (as though they were inspectors). There is no question of their examining and inspecting us, reviewing and judging us. Of asking us for an account; of their asking us: that really would be a bit much. The only right they have is the right to keep quiet. And of trying to be forgotten. Let us hope they will make good use of it.

What I maintain is that the whole mystical body of Dreyfusism remained intact. Who cares whether the politicians betrayed the *mystique?* It is their office to do so.

"Then," you will say, "neither the General Staff nor the various Committees, nor the Leagues, belonged to the *mystique.*" Of course not. You surely did not expect them to. What does the League of the Rights of Man, and even of the Citizen, matter, what does it stand for by comparison with a conscience, a *mystique?* What does a policy, or a hundred policies matter by comparison with a *mystique? Mystiques* are always the creditors of policies.

You will add that the victim himself did not belong to the *mystique.* To his own *mystique.* That has become clear. We would have died for Dreyfus. Dreyfus did not die for Dreyfus. It is quite a good rule that the victim should not belong to the *mystique* of his own affair.

There you have the triumph of human weakness, the crown of our vanity, the supreme proof; the great masterpiece and demonstration of our infirmity.

It had to be so, in order that the masterpiece of our misery should be complete, in order that the bitterness should be drunk to the dregs, and ingratitude crowned.

So that it should be complete. In order that the disillusionment should be complete.

There is no doubt whatsoever, as far as we are concerned, the Dreyfusist *mystique* was not only a particular instance of the Christian *mystique,* but an outstanding example, an acceleration, a crisis, a temporal crisis, a sort of transition, which I should describe as necessary. Why deny it, now that we are twelve or fifteen years distant from our youth, and that we at last see clear in our hearts? Our Dreyfusism was a religion; I use the word in the most exact and literal sense, a religious impulse, a religious crisis, and I should even advise anyone who wanted to consider, study and know a religious movement in modern times, to take that unique example, so clearly defined, so full of character. I would add that for us, that religious movement was essentially Christian, Christian in origin, growing from a Christian stem, deriving from an ancient source. To that we can now bear witness. The Justice and the Truth which we have loved so much, to which we gave everything, our youth, to which we gave ourselves completely during the whole of our youth, were not an abstract, conceptual Justice and Truth, they were not a dead justice and a dead truth, the justice and truth found in books and libraries, a notional, intellectual justice and truth, the justice and truth of the intellectual party; they were organic, Christian, in no sense modern, they were eternal and not temporal only, they were Justice and Truth, a living Justice and a living Truth. And of all the feelings which impelled us, in fear and trembling, into that unique crisis, we can now admit that of all the passions that drove us into that seething, boiling tumult, into that furnace, there was at the heart of them one virtue, and that virtue was charity. And I do not want to reopen an old quarrel, an argument that has become historical, historic; nevertheless, among our enemies, our enemies of those days, I can see a great deal of intelligence, a great deal of lucidity and even much shrewdness and sharpness, but what strikes me most is certainly a certain lack of charity. I do not want to anticipate what belongs properly speaking to *confessions*. But it is undeniable that in all our socialism there was infinitely more Christianity than in the whole of the Madeleine together with Saint-Pierre de Chaillot and Saint-Philippe du Roule and Saint-Honoré d'Eylau. It was essentially a religion of temporal poverty. It is therefore the religion which will never be acclaimed in any way in modern times. The very last to be celebrated with a holiday. We were marked by it, indelibly marked, and received its imprint so deeply that we shall be marked by it for the rest of our temporal lives, and for the other too. Our socialism was never a parliamentary socialism, nor the socialism of a rich parish. Our Christianity will never be a parliamentary Christianity, nor the Christianity of a rich parish. We received, from that time on, a vocation marked by poverty, by want even, deep, inward and at the same time so historical, so full of emergencies and contingencies, that we have never been able to escape from it, and that I begin to believe that no one ever will be able to extricate us from it.

It is a sort of vocation.

A destination.

What may have deceived people is that all the political forces of the Church were against Dreyfusism. But the political forces of the Church have always been against its *mystique*. Particularly against the Christian *mystique*. That is the supreme illustration of the general rule laid down above.

One might even say that the Dreyfus Affair was a *perfect example* of a religious movement, of the beginning or origin of a religion, a rare case and perhaps a unique one.

In fact, the Dreyfusist *mystique* was, for us, essentially a crisis in the French *mystique*. For us, and through us, the Affair was very definitely in the direct French line. Just as for us and through us, it was in the Christian line. We ourselves were situated very exactly in the French line, just as we had been in the Christian line. We were in it in our character as Frenchmen, just as we were in it in our character as Christians.

We deployed the French virtues, the French qualities, the virtues of the race: a lucid courage, speed, good humor, firmness, constancy and an obstinate courage, but of a decent, well-behaved kind: fanatical, and at the same time measured; passionate but full of sense; a cheerful sadness typical of the French; a deliberate purpose; a resolution at once cold and heated; a constant freedom and intelligence; docility in face of the event and at the same time a perpetual revolt against it;

an organic incapacity to consent to injustice. A supple, subtle blade. The point well sharpened. More simply, we were heroes. More precisely, French heroes. (The proof is that we have not recovered, that we did not withdraw. We shall be on half-pay all our lives perhaps.) In fact, it is essential to see what the question was. Where we were concerned, the question was never whether Dreyfus was innocent or guilty. But whether people would have the courage or not have the courage to declare and to know him to be innocent.

When we write our history of the Dreyfus Affair, which will properly speaking be the *Memoirs of a Dreyfusist,* we shall have to examine and study very closely, and we shall have to establish in great detail, what I would call *the curve of public belief in the innocence of Dreyfus.* The curve naturally underwent the most extraordinary variations. Naturally too, the anti-Dreyfusists did everything in their power to make it *rise,* and one must be just to the Dreyfusists and admit that they generally speaking did everything possible to make it *fall.* Starting from about zero in 1894 (the family and certain rare individuals excepted), one may say that it rose, that it underwent all the political and historical fluctuations which never fail to affect these sorts of curves, and that after all manner of jumps and changes, it rose regularly up to the day when they brought Dreyfus back to France and introduced among us the real substance of the dispute. From that time on, in spite of appearances, in spite of a temporary equilibrium, when it was apparently horizontal, it really began to fall, slowly and surely. In spite of changing luck, in spite of apparent good fortune, it began, in reality, to fall. That decline, that fall, that collapse has now ceased, and one may say that it has ceased forever, because it can hardly fall lower, because many people nowadays laugh at the whole thing, and above all because we have again reached a state of equilibrium, a very seductive equilibrium, very stable and conventional, where we remained for so long a time at the moment of the rise: France, the world, history, cut in two, into two perfectly distinct parties, clear-cut, clearly delineated, believing professionally, officially, the one in culpability and the other in innocence. That is the usual situation, the ordinary, common or garden situation, the classical situation, the well-known situation: the world divided on a question. The most comfortable situation imaginable, because it means war, the situation of mutual hate. The situation everyone is accustomed to. And that is why it will last, why it threatened to last even during the rise of the curve and why it has been rediscovered again at the same level on the way down, at the same point in the decline of the curve, and will not be lost again but will be definitive. Allowing for successive petrifactions, naturally, and the arrival of successive generations; allowing for increasing petrifaction and final extinction, historical extinction.

What is remarkable is the convenience of that situation, that intermediary level, with the country split in two; how complacently, how comfortably we stopped there on the way up, during the rise, how easily and quickly we settled there again on the way down. Comfortably. But what cannot be denied is that in the course of its sudden fall, and during the course of its rise, the curve attained to a *maximum* on several occasions, to a maximum which was a sort of *universum*. What I mean is that in the course of these fluctuations, agitations, crises, there were at least two or three occasions when for forty-eight hours the *whole* country (our adversaries and even their leaders) believed in the innocence of Dreyfus. Particularly, for example, after the thunderbolt, immediately after the theatrical coup of Colonel Henry's death (in Mont Valérien), or pretended death, assassination, murder, suicide or faked suicide. (His disappearance in fact.) How we fell back and redescended from that *summum*, which on that day, in that lightning stroke, seemed definitely to have been attained; how we were made to descend again, how the curve was brought down again, is the secret of the politicians. The secret of politics itself. The secret of Dreyfus himself, to the extent to which, and it is total, he left us and placed himself entirely in the hands of the politicians. How they managed to win the bet and make us fall from that *maximum* is their secret and the secret of their great skill. Ask Jaurès how one loses a battle already won.

When our enemies and our adversaries reproached us with being the foreign party, they were totally and absolutely wrong about us and against us (about our *mystique* and against our *mystique*); they were partly right about and against our General Staff, which in fact masked us from them, and which really did everything in its power to conceal us from the world, and succeeded almost perfectly in doing so; they were partly right (to the extent of about one-third) about and against our leaders, about and against our policy, our politicians; and, in fact, they had the right not to recognize us in the confusion and medley of the fight, and strictly speaking they may never have recognized us. The fair on the market square could very well have concealed the inside of the house; they may only have seen the political parade; and at worst, at the most, when our enemies and adversaries accuse us of being the foreign party, the party of foreigners, they could only do us temporal harm; an extreme temporal harm, a capital harm, but, when all is said and done, a temporal harm. They could not dishonor us. They might make us lose our worldly goods, they might make us lose liberty, they could make us lose our lives, and the soil of our country. They could not make us lose honor.

But when Jaurès, on the one hand, through his cowardly and suspect subservience to Hervé personally and to Hervé-ism, allowed it to be said, in regard to France, that one had to deny and destroy France, and even allowed it to be done;[9] thus creating the political illusion that the Dreyfusist movement was an anti-French movement; and when on the other hand, in regard to the Faith, and moved by base electoral interest, impelled by a low and cowardly subservience to the radical agitators and demagogues, he said and so acted that the Dreyfus Affair and Dreyfusism was involved in the demagogy, in the radical agitation, the anticlerical, anti-Catholic, anti-Christian agitation, in the separation of Church and State, in the law against the Religious Congregations (Waldeck-Rousseau's) and in the strange application of that law by Combes; thus creating a political illusion that the Dreyfusist movement was anti-Christian; he not only succeeded in betraying us, he not only made us deviate, he dishonored us.

It must never be forgotten that Combism, the Combist system, the Combes tyranny, the source of all our ills, was Jaurès's invention, that it was Jaurès with his detestable political power, with his oratorical power, with his parliamentary

9. By allowing the Radicals under Combes to divide and weaken France and particularly the Army, by pursuing their anti-Catholic policy. Hervé was a pacifist, no recommendation in Péguy's eyes, which were firmly fixed on the war to come.

power, who imposed that invention, that tyranny on the country, that dominion, that he alone maintained it and could maintain it; and that for three and even four years he was the veritable master of the Republic under the name of M. Combes. Bernard-Lazare had seen at once with his great *political* lucidity, that they had not even waited for the end of the Dreyfus Affair, for the conclusion, to begin operating the contamination, the degeneration, the dishonor and deviation and degradation of the *mystique* into a *politique;* for it was between the two Dreyfus Affairs, that they were preparing to commit the operation, to accomplish it, even before having liquidated the Affair, at the very moment when they were preparing to open it again (which means to say that they had begun the operation of degrading the *mystique* into a *politique* at the very moment when they were preparing to call once again on all the forces, all the incalculable forces of the *mystique*).

That is why our politicians were the worst criminals, criminals in the second degree. If they had simply carried out their policy, professionally so to speak, if they had only followed their trade as politicians, they might only be culpable in the first degree. But they wanted at the same time to retain all the advantages of the *mystique*. And that is precisely what constitutes the second degree. They not only wanted to betray the *mystique* and at the same time not only claim it as theirs, not only clothe themselves in it, use it and appear in it, but continue to inflame it. They wanted and meant to play a double game, they wanted to bet on both colors simultaneously, on both odds, both the mystical, and the political which excludes the mystical, they wanted to back *their* policy and *our mys-*

tique, gaining the advantage of their policy and of our *mystique,* backing the temporal and the eternal.

That is what makes Jaurès's responsibility in that crime, in that double crime, that crime of the second degree, so great. He of all men, the head of the operation, was a politician among others, a trimmer among trimmers; but he pretended not to be a politician. Hence his supreme responsibility. When the professional nationalists said that we were *the foreign party* they simply libeled us, they could only do us a temporal harm, an extreme temporal harm. But when Jaurès spoke for us, on our behalf, and linked the Dreyfus Affair and Dreyfusism to the antipatriotic political party, the antipatriotic Hervéism, confused it with the Hervéist agitation and demagogy, the anti-Christian demagogy, he reached, touched and wounded the very heart of Dreyfusism.

Jaurès's culminating responsibility in that double crime was that he, of all others, was a politician, like the rest of them, and that he claimed to be a mystic. He would of course argue like the casuist, the dealer he is, and really I don't know of anyone who is quite such a horse-coper. But he knows quite well what we mean.

By his whole university past, his intellectual past, his early university career, by his relationships, by the whole tone of the man, by the friendships, the sheaf of *ardent* friendships which formed around him and which he complacently encouraged, friendships of the poor, of little people, of professors, of ourselves, and which he seemed to sum up in himself to focus as a hearth focuses light and warmth — all this made Jaurès into a figure, a sort of professor delegated among politicians, an intellectual, a philosopher (in those days all the *agrégés de philosophie* were philosophers just as they are all sociologists now); gave him the figure of a man who worked, who knew what it meant to work. Who had a trade. The figure he cut was essentially that of a nonpolitical man, a man who was charged, as it were, to represent us, to translate us into politics. On the contrary, he was a politician who had pretended to be a professor, who had pretended to be an intellectual, who had pretended to work and to know how to work, to have a trade, who had pretended to be one of us, who had made a pretense of everything. There is nothing to be said against those who carry on the trade of politics, the profession of politics, nothing to be said when they perform and function officially, under their right name, as politicians. But when those who make a business and a profession of being nonpolitical play politics under that name, there is a double crime, a double deceit. To be a politician and to call oneself a politician is as it should be. But to indulge in politics and call it a *mystique,* to take a *mystique* and turn it into politics is an unforgivable deceit. To steal from the poor is to steal twice. To deceive the simple is to deceive twice over. To steal the most precious thing of all, belief. Confidence. And God knows we were simple souls, poor insignificant men. That is what makes them laugh nowadays. "*Who,*" they say, "*who are the fools who believed what I said?*" But they need not worry, they only have to wait. Life is long, movements change, and it might be as well if they did not fall into our hands. Perhaps they would not go on laughing.

What could be more poignant than Bernard-Lazare's testimony, than the words of the man already condemned and destined (to death); what could be more redoubtable than his testimony, redoubtable in its very moderation? "When Jaurès," Bernard-Lazare wrote, "comes before us to defend a work he approves, in which he wants us to collaborate, he must, being Jaurès, being our companion in a battle not yet finished, give us other reasons besides theological ones." (He saw quite clearly that there was a lot of crude theology in Jaurès, in all that modern *mentality*, in that political, parliamentary radicalism, in that pseudo-metaphysic, in that pseudo-philosophy, in that sociology.) Moreover, it was certainly giving a theological reason to say (and here I must warn the reader that Bernard-Lazare is quoting some Jaurès: " 'There are political and social crimes which do not go unpaid, and the great collective crime committed by the Church against the truth, against humanity, against the law and against the Republic is at last going to receive its fair wage. Not in vain did it revolt consciences through its complicity with falsehood, perjury and betrayal.' " Bernard-Lazare said more simply: "One should not nag at people because they say their prayers." He was a man who knew the ways of liberty. He had it in his blood, in his bones. Not an intellectual, conceptual, bookish liberty, a ready-made library liberty. A codified liberty. But a primitive, organic, living liberty. I have never seen a man believe to that degree, never seen a man with such a degree of certitude, such conscious realization, that the human conscience was absolute, invincible, eternal and free, such certainty that it could victoriously oppose and eternally triumph over the powers of this world. "One must not accept justifications of that order," Bernard-Lazare wrote, "even and especially when they are given by Jaurès, because others lower than him are only waiting to interpret them in a worse sense, and to draw consequences *dangerous to liberty.*" He enumerated, quoting examples, in a striking, cutting, terse style, some of the principal antinomies, some of the contradictions. He foresaw *the resistance of the Polish people to the exactions of Prussian Germanization.* And in fact he wrote at the time, and his words are as clear, as important and as actual as on the first day: "*If we do not take care, we shall very soon find ourselves applauding the French Gendarme who takes a child by the arm and forces him to go to the Lay School, while reproving the Prussian Gendarme for using force on a Polish schoolboy in Wreschen.*" That is the man, the friend we have lost. Again he wrote, and his words deserve to be pondered, as carefully as when they were written: "*Give us a proposal for solving the school question and we will discuss it. But as from today one can say that a state monopoly is not the solution.* WE REFUSE TO ACCEPT DOGMAS FORMULATED BY THE TEACHING STATE QUITE AS MUCH AS THE DOGMAS FORMULATED BY THE CHURCH. WE HAVE NO MORE CONFIDENCE IN THE UNIVERSITY THAN IN THE TEACHING ORDERS." But I must stop quoting him. After all, I cannot quote the whole of that admirable report, quote a whole *Cahier* in a *Cahier*, rewrite *Cahiers* in *Cahiers*, put the whole of III.21 into XI.12.

That is the man, the friend we have lost. We shall never make an apology for a man like that, we will never put up with people writing one.

Those are the men who count, the only ones who count. It is we who count, we alone who count. Not only have the others no right to speak for us. It is we who have to speak for all.

He was a hero, and, moreover, there was a large element of sanctity in him. And we, with him, were, obscurely, heroes.

Nor can anyone help noting in the few words we have quoted, in those few phrases that we have reported, I cannot refrain from noting, not only the sense of liberty and the ease with which he moves within liberty, his easy handling of liberty, but that much more curious sense, the much more unexpected, seemingly unexpected, awareness of theology. Suddenly he saw it burgeoning everywhere, where in fact it shows, it or an imitation of it, itself or a counterfeit.

How can anyone avoid noting, too, his precise, his perfect, his real internationalism, Israel excepted, the exactitude, the ease of his internationalism, which was taken for granted, which was much too simple, too natural, nothing forced, learnt, bookish, much too natural to be antinationalism? When he referred to the Poles in defending the Bretons, it was not as a joke, as an amusing comparison. It was not a clever, witty thing to say, a good joke. It was because he naturally saw the Bretons and the Poles on the same level. He really saw Christianity as the same as Islam, which none of us, even those who most wished to do so, could achieve. Because he was really equally outside both. A view, an angle, which none of us could achieve. At the time when they were doing everything, even and perhaps especially in his own circle, everything humanly possible to evict his Jews from Romania, for political reasons, in order not to compromise and complicate the Armenian movement, he saw perfectly clearly through the intentional clouding of the issues, the darkening of counsel, and when an old friend, who lived in the same quarter, left him, he said softly, gently shrugging his shoulders as he used to do, showing the matter to me, as it were, with his shoulders, over the top of his shoulders: "He is trying," he said, "to trick me again with his Armenians. It's always the same. They take . . . on . . . the Grand Turk, because he is a Turk, and they don't want one single word said about the King of Romania, because he is a Christian. There is always the same collusion among Christians."

How can one fail to notice, to observe, how well he always wrote; so measured, assured, clear, noble, so *French*. "One must not accept *justifications of that order*."

Apologia for Bernard-Lazare. Nourished, fed on our *mystique*, quickly deforming and degrading it, turning it at once into a *politique*, our politicians, Jaurès at their head, Jaurès first and foremost, created a double illusion, first of all that Dreyfusism was anti-Christian, and secondly that it was anti-French. The second calls for a moment's pause.

Our socialism, our original socialism need I say, was not in the least anti-French, not in the least antipatriotic, not in the least *anti*national. It was rigorously, precisely, *inter*national. Theoretically it was not in the least antinational. It was quite definitely international. Far from reducing or weakening the race, it exalted it, strengthened it. On the contrary, our thesis was, and still is, that, on the contrary, it is the bourgeoisie, bourgeois capitalism, capitalist sabotage, bourgeois and capitalist sabotage, which wiped out nation and people. It should be realized that there was nothing in common between the socialism of those days and the thing we know under that name today. Here again politics have done their work, and nowhere have politics undone and altered the nature of the *mystique* so completely as in this instance. The politics, I say, of the professional politicians, of the parliamentary politicians. But it has done still more, without a doubt, through the invention, the intervention, interpolation of sabotage, which is a political invention, in the same sense as the vote, *more political still than the vote,* worse, by which I mean more political; more even, without a doubt, than the professional antipoliticians, the syndicalists, the antiparliamentarians. We thought then and we still think, though fifteen years ago everyone thought as we did, or affected to do so, that there was not a shadow of doubt, not a suggestion of disagreement on that point, that principle. It is quite obvious that it was the bourgeois and the capitalist who began it. I mean to say, the bourgeois and the capitalist ceased to perform their office, their social task, before the working man, long before the working man stopped doing his. There can be no doubt about it: sabotage came from above, and the bourgeois and capitalist sabotage antedates sabotage from below; the bourgeois and the capitalist stopped loving bourgeois and capitalist work long before the working men stopped loving their work. It is in that order, beginning with the bourgeois capitalist world, that the general turning away from work occurred; the deepest stain, the central stain on the modern world, this aversion from work. Such is the general situation in the modern world; there was no question, as our syndicalist politicians like to pretend, of inventing, *adding* the disorder of the working-class to the disorder of the bourgeoisie, working-class sabotage to bourgeois and capitalist disorder. *On the contrary,* our socialism was essentially, and officially moreover, a theory, a general theory, a doctrine and method, a philosophy of organization and of the reorganization of work, the *restoration* of work. Our socialism was essentially, and moreover officially, a restoration, a general and even universal restoration. Nobody at the time contested the fact. But the politicians have been on the move for fifteen years. Two kinds of politicians, the politicians strictly speaking, and the antipoliticians. The politicians have passed on. What was at stake was a general restoration, beginning with the working-class world. A total restoration founded on the previous restoration of the world of the worker. It was a matter, and no one contested it at the time, on the contrary they all taught it, it was very definitely a matter of making the world of the worker in general healthy, of restoring the whole city to health, organically and atomically, beginning with the individual. That was the method and the ethics and the general philosophy of M. Sorel, himself a moralist and philosopher, which found its highest expression in his work. I add that it could be nothing else.

There can be no question of its being anything else. Let us say it without mincing our words. To the philosopher, and to any man philosophizing, our socialism was a religion of temporal salvation, and nothing less. In seeking to restore health to the world of the worker, by restoring health to work and the world of work, by giving work back its dignity, and restoring the whole economic and industrial world, we were seeking nothing short of the temporal salvation of humanity. That is what we call the industrial world as opposed to the intellectual and political world, the world of learning, the parliamentary world; that is what we call *economics;* the morale of the producer; industrial morale; the world of producers; the economic world, the world of the working man; the (organic and molecular) structure, economic and industrial; that is what we call industry, the industrial régime, industrial production. The intellectual and political world, on the contrary, and the learned and parliamentary world belong together. By restoring health to the factory we hoped for no less, we aimed at no less than the temporal salvation of humanity. A joke only to those who do not want to see that Christianity, the religion of eternal salvation, is bogged down in the mud of rotten economic and industrial morals; and that it cannot extricate itself, will not get free, except at the price of an economic and industrial revolution; for in fact there is nowhere, no place better conceived, no source of perdition better organized and fitted out, so to say, no instrument better adapted to perdition than a modern factory.

All the Church's difficulties stem from the point; all its real, profound, popular difficulties: from the fact that in spite of some so-called works among the working-class, under the cloak of some so-called social workers, and a few so-called Catholic workers, the factory is closed to the Church and the Church to the factory; that in the modern world, it too has suffered a modernization, has become the religion, almost solely the religion of the rich, and is no longer, if I may so express it, socially the communion of the faithful. The whole weakness, and perhaps one ought to say the growing weakness of the Church in the modern world does not come, as people think, from the fact that Science has constructed systems against religion which are said to be invincible, or that Science has discovered arguments against religion said to be victorious, but from the fact that what remains of the Christian world is lacking today, profoundly lacking, in charity. It is not arguments that are wanting. It is charity. All the arguments, all the systems, all the pseudo-scientific arguments would be as nothing, would weigh nothing, if there were an ounce of charity. All those intellectual attitudes would not make much impression, if Christendom had remained what it was, a religion of the heart. That is one of the reasons why the moderns understand nothing about Christianity, true, real, historical Christianity. (And how many Christians any longer understand anything about it? How many Christians are there who are not modern even on that point, on that point too?) They believe, when they are sincere, and such do exist, they believe that Christianity was always modern, more precisely that it was such as they see it in the modern world, where there is no longer a Christendom, in the sense in which there was one. And so, whichever way one takes it, everything in the modern world is modern, and the neatest shot of all no doubt is to have made Christianity itself, the Church and what is left of Christendom, modern in so many, in almost all, senses. When there is an eclipse, everyone is in the dark. Everything that happens in an age, everything that passes through an epoch or enters a period, a zone, everything that exists in a world and is placed in a place, in a time, in a world, and is situated in a certain situation, a temporal situation, is colored by it or bears the mark of its shadow.

There has been a lot of fuss about a certain intellectual modernism which is not even a heresy, but a form of modern intellectual poverty, the residue, the dregs of the bottle, the lees of the barrel, a modern intellectual impoverishment of the great heresies of the past "for moderns." That modern poverty would not have ravaged the countryside, it would only have been ridiculous, if its path had not been prepared, if there had not been that infinitely grave modernism of the heart, that infinitely serious modernism of charity. If its path had not been prepared by that modernism of the heart and of charity. That is the reason why the Church in the modern world, why Christendom in the modern world, is no longer of the people, which it once was, that it is no longer so in any sense; that it is no longer a people socially, an immense people, an immense race; that Christianity is no longer the religion, socially, of the depths, a people's religion, a religion of the people, a common religion, of a whole people, temporal, eternal, a religion rooted in the temporal depths themselves, the religion of a race, of a whole temporal race, an eternal race; and that it is only a religion of the bourgeois, of the rich, a superior sort of religion for the upper, superior, classes of society, of the nation, a miserable sort of refined religion for refined people, and consequently everything that is most superficial, artificial and the opposite of profound; inexistent; everything that is wretched and miserably formal; and, moreover, everything that is most contrary to its institution; to the sanctity, the poverty, and even to the very form of its institution. To the truth, letter and spirit of its institution. Its own institution. One only has to look at the least of the Gospel texts.

It is enough to refer to what it is better to call, in a single word, the Gospel.

It is spiritual poverty and misery, and temporal riches, which have done everything, which have done the harm. That modernism of the heart, the modernism of charity itself, has caused the failure and collapse in the Church, in Christianity, in Christendom itself, which has brought about the degradation of the *mystique* into a *politique*.

A lot of fuss is being made about the fact that since the Separation,[10] Catholicism, Christianity, is no longer the official religion of the State, and that therefore the Church is free. In a sense, people are right. The position of the Church is clearly quite different under the new *régime*. Under the severe discipline of liberty, and by a certain poverty, the Church has found a new self under the new *régime*. Under the new *régime* we shall never again get Bishops quite as bad as the Bishops of the Concordat period. But one must not exaggerate either. One must not conceal the fact that while the Church has ceased to act as the official religion of the State, it has not ceased to act as the official religion of the bourgeoisie in the State. Politically, she has cast off the burdens involved by her official position, but socially she has not cast them off. That is why

10. The abrogation of the Concordat in 1905 which had governed the relations of Church and State since 1801.

there is no reason to claim a victory. That is why the factory is still closed to the Church, and the Church to the factory. She acts as, and is, the official formal religion of the rich. That is what the people, obscurely or explicitly, very certainly feel quite well. That is what they see. She is therefore nothing; that is why she is nothing. And above all, she is unlike what she was, having become all that is most contrary to herself, to her institution. And she will not reopen the factory doors, she will not reopen the way to the people except by *bearing the cost* of a revolution, an economic, social, industrial revolution, and, to call a spade a spade, a *temporal* revolution for *eternal* salvation. Such is, eternally, temporally (eternally temporally, and temporally eternally), the mysterious subjection of the eternal itself to the temporal. Such, properly speaking, is the inscription of the eternal itself on the temporal. The economic, social and industrial price must be paid, the temporal price. Nothing can evade it, not even the eternal, not even the spiritual, not even the inward life. That is why our socialism was not so stupid after all, and why it was profoundly Christian.

That is why you only have to put the old Christendom under their noses,[11] under their eyes, and show them what a Christian parish was in reality, a French parish at the beginning of the fifteenth century, at a time when there were French parishes, and make them see what Christendom was in reality, in the days when there was a Christendom, and what a great Saint was like, the greatest of all perhaps, in an age when there were saints, at a time when there was such a thing as *charity*,

11. This refers to *The Mystery of the Charity of Joan of Arc.*

when there were saints and holy women, a whole Christian people, a whole world of saints and sinners, and immediately some of your modern Catholics, modern in spite of themselves, without boasting of it, intellectual in spite of themselves, but not boasting of it, intellectual nevertheless, deeply intellectual, intellectuals to the very marrow of their bones, bourgeois and sons of bourgeois, *rentiers* and sons of *rentiers*, retired civil servants, pensioned by the State, civil servants, pensioned by others, by other citizens, other electors, and who ingeniously manage to get inscribed on the Great Book of the Public Debt, the guarantees, modest enough, of their daily bread, and thus armed, some of these contemporary Catholics, faced by the sudden revelation of an age-old Christendom, cry out as though their modesty had been outraged.[12] If need be they would deny Joinville as too coarse, too common, too much of the people. The Lord of Joinville. And perhaps they would deny Saint Louis. For being too much a King of France.

The temporal price must be paid. That is to say that no one (not even the Church, or whatever spiritual power it may be) can extricate himself except by, or for less than, a temporal revolution. Except by paying the price. In order not to pay, in order to avoid paying, there has been a singular agreement, a curious collusion between the Church and the intellectual party. It would be amusing, it would even be ridiculous, if it were not profoundly sad. That accord, that collusion con-

12. Péguy's outburst was prompted by the failure of the Catholics to appreciate *The Mystery of the Charity of Joan of Arc* and by the silly criticisms which certain Catholic intellectuals made of his freedom in speaking of sacred things.

sists in displacing and in rearranging the dispute, the very ground of the argument. The object of the dispute. In concealing that modernism of the heart, that modernism of charity, and throwing into relief, into false relief, into the light, into a false light, and so exposing to view, intellectual modernism, the whole apparatus of intellectual modernism, its solemn, pompous apparatus. In that way everyone is the gainer, for it costs nothing, it does not cost a revolution whether economic, industrial, social or temporal; and the bourgeois on both sides, the capitalists on either side, of either confession, the clericals and the radicals, the radical clericals and the clerical radicals, the intellectuals and the clerks, the intellectual clerks and the clerical intellectuals, desire nothing so much, long for nothing so much as: *not to pay*. Not to foot the bill. Not to incur the expense. Not to fork out. If I may be forgiven so crude an expression. Though it is almost unavoidable in such a crude situation. A truly wonderful concert, a really admirable collusion. Everyone gains everything. Not only does it cost nothing, but there is, naturally, the fame and the glory, thrown in, that only comes to those who deserve it. Everyone gets his deserts, and even ours. Once again the two opposing parties are in agreement, find themselves, put themselves, in agreement, not only with the intention of falsifying the dispute which divides them or appears to divide them, by transposing the very ground of the dispute to where the dispute costs least and profits them most, where the advantages are greatest, driven solely by the consideration of their temporal interests. The operation consists in effacing, in keeping that terrifying modernism of the heart in the shade, and of putting intellectual modernism first, in the first and only place, and attributing everything that happens to the terrifying power, the supposedly colossal power of intellectual modernism. A substitution, a really wonderful transposition. The intellectuals are of course enchanted. "*Look,*" they exclaim, "*look at what power we have. What brains we have. We have found arguments, reasons, such amazing reasons, that alone and by themselves they have shaken the Faith.* And the proof that it's true is *that the priests themselves say so.*" And the priests, together with the good clerical bourgeois, supposedly Catholic, claiming to be Christian, forgetful of the anathemas, the terrifying anathemas and curses on the rich and on money in which the Gospels are saturated, comfortably ensconced in their peace of mind, in a social peace, both together cry out: "Everything," they wail, "everything is the fault of those damn' Professors who have discovered and invented such arguments, such amazing logical reasons. And the *proof of it all is that we, the priests, say so.*" Then all goes hummingly, and not only everyone is in the Republic, everyone is happy. Purses remain in pockets, and the money remains in the purses. No one has to put their hands in their pockets. That's the point. But I repeat: all those arguments would not weigh much, if there were an ounce of charity.

The clerical bourgeois affect to believe that it is the arguments, that it is cerebral modernism which is important, simply in order not to have to pay for an industrial revolution, an economic revolution.

Such being our socialism, and it being no secret, it is clear that it did not and could not endanger the legitimate rights of nations, but being and involving a general purification and restoration to health, could but serve the most essential interests of the nation and the legitimate rights of the people, within that process of restoration. The most sacred rights and interests. And it alone did so. It did not violate or obliterate nations and peoples; it did not force or falsify them, or twist them; on the contrary it worked to bring about a substitution, to replace the anarchic competition of nations with a growing forest of prosperous peoples, a whole world of flourishing peoples. It was not a denial of nations and of peoples. On the contrary it implied founding them, bringing them to birth and making them grow. It meant *making* them. From that moment we knew, we were certain that the world suffered infinitely more from bourgeois capitalist sabotage than from the sabotage of the working class. Contrary to what is generally believed, to what the intellectual and the bourgeois believe, to what publicists and sociologists believe, sabotage in the working man's world did not originate in this working man's world. It did not come from below, rising up from the mud, from the depths of the working man's world. It comes from above. Socialism is the only thing that can avoid it, avoid that contamination. It is bourgeois sabotage that, little by little, has extended down through all levels, down into the world of the working man. It is not his own peculiar vices which are gradually poisoning his world. It is his world which is gradually becoming bourgeois. Contrary to what is thought, sabotage is not innate, is not native to the worker. It is learned. Taught dogmatically, intellectually, like a foreign language. It is a bourgeois invention. It meets with a resistance which is never met with in the bourgeois world. It has not won the battle. The city is not taken. And it remains, all things considered, artificial. It comes up against the most unforeseen

resistance, resistance that goes incredibly deep, to that perennial love of work which enriches the hard-working heart. The
capitalist and bourgeois world is almost entirely, almost completely, given up to pleasure. One can still find a large number
of working men, and not only among the old, who *love* work.

Such being our socialism, it is clear that it implied, that it
meant the restoration of health to the nation and the people, a
strengthening hitherto unknown, prosperity, flowering, fer-
tility. . . .

Thus the world of the working man followed a path exactly
opposite to the one we desired, for as a result of sabotage the
working man became a bourgeois. We wanted to restore their
world to health, and rising step by step, to strengthen and
cure the bourgeois world, and thus the whole of society, the
city itself. The opposite happened. Far from wanting to add
disorder to disorder, we wanted to install, to restore order, a
new, an old order; ancient and new; never modern; a hard-
working order; and by infection so to speak, rising gradually
up the scale, to restore order to disorder. In fact, the infection
descended and resulted in disorder infecting order. It disorga-
nized the organism, the organization. But we have the right
to say that that disorder, that bad example, was introduced
into the world of the artisan by a sort of intellectual insertion,
as the result of an operation as artificial as, for example, the
invention of the People's Universities.

Thus the whole tension of the modern world, its whole tendency, is toward money and the whole drag toward money

ends by contaminating the Christian world itself, causes it to sacrifice its faith and its morals for the sake of maintaining economic and social peace.

That, properly speaking, is modernism of the heart, modernism of charity, modernism of morals.

There are two kinds of rich: the atheist rich, who being *rich* understand nothing about religion. So they set about explaining the history of comparative religions, and indeed excel at it (and to be fair, they have done everything not to make it a history of *religion*). It is they who invented the *science* of comparative religions; And there are the pious rich, who being *rich* understand nothing about Christianity. And so they profess it.

Such is, and one must not blink the fact, one must face up to it, such is the terrifying modernism of the modern world; its terrifying, miserable efficacy. It has wounded, succeeded in wounding, in modernizing, Christendom itself. It has made Christianity itself, in charity and in morals, suspect.

Need I say, need I note, for the sake of order, need I recall how truly that socialism of ours was in the pure French tradition? The French vocation, destination, the French office, has always been to enlighten and give health to the world. To give health to what is sick, to enlighten what is troubled, to give order to what is disordered, to organize what is inchoate. Is it necessary to note the extent to which our socialism was based on generosity, how clear that generosity was, how full and pure and in the French tradition? In the sap and in the race itself. In the sap and in the blood of the race. A generosity at once abundant and sober, generous and well balanced, full, pure, fertile, clear, delicate, exuberant yet not giddy, well balanced but not sterile. In fact, a heroism at once sober, gay and prudent, a French heroism.

We were heroes. One must say it quite simply, for I really do not think anyone will say it for us. And here, very exactly, is how and why we were heroes. In the world in which we moved, where we were completing our years of apprenticeship, in all the circles in which we moved and worked, the question which was asked, during those two or three years of the rising curve, was never whether Dreyfus was *in reality* innocent (or guilty). The question was whether one could have the courage to recognize and to declare his innocence. To proclaim his innocence. Whether one had the double courage. First of all the first courage, the outward, crude courage, difficult enough in itself, the social courage to proclaim him innocent publicly, to testify publicly to him. To bet on it, to risk everything, to *put* everything one had on him, all one's miserable gains, the little man's money, the money of the poor; to put time, life and career on him; health, the heartbreak of family feuds, the quarrels with one's nearest friends, the averted gaze, the silent or violent reprobation; the isolation, the quarantine; friendships of twenty years' standing broken, which meant, for us, friendships that had always been. The whole of social life. One's whole life in fact, everything. Secondly, the second courage, more difficult still, the inward courage, the secret courage, to admit to oneself in oneself that he was innocent. To give up one's peace of mind for the sake of that man.

Not only the peace of the city, the peace of one's home. The peace of one's family and household. But the peace of one's heart.

To the supreme good, the only good.

The courage to enter the kingdom of an incurable unrest for the sake of this man.

And of a bitterness that would never be cured.

Our adversaries will never know, they could not know what we have sacrificed for him, or how that sacrifice came from the heart. We sacrificed our whole life to him, for that Affair marked us for life. Our enemies will never know how few we were, we who overturned and changed the country, they will never guess the conditions in which we were fighting, what precarious, miserable, ungrateful conditions we were in. And in consequence the extent to which, in order to win, since after all we did win, we had to deploy and reveal and rediscover in ourselves, in our race, the oldest and most precious qualities of the race. The very technique of heroism, and notably of military heroism. One must not boggle over words. The *discipline* of the *anarchists*, for example, was admirable. It cannot have escaped the notice of any perceptive onlooker that the military virtues were on our side. In us, and not in the General Staff of the Army. We were, once more, that handful of Frenchmen under a crushing fire, breaking through sheer masses, carrying the assault, carrying the position.

How should our enemies, how should our adversaries know it, when our friends (I mean those of our party, on our side, the politicians, the historians of our side), when our friends even do not notice it? And on the question of anarchists, for example, don't ask them for information about themselves. They would swear by all their gods, if I may so express it, that they were never so undisciplined. People are so intellectualist that they prefer to betray themselves, to forsake and deny their own history and their own reality and everything that constitutes their value, their greatness, rather than give up their formulas, their *tics*, their little intellectual manias, the intellectual idea they like to have of themselves, and that they want others to have of them.

The theoreticians of the *Action Française* insist that the Dreyfus Affair, in its principle and origin, was not only a pernicious, shoddy affair, but an intellectual affair, an intellectual construction, an invention: an intellectual plot. I shall allow myself to say, in my turn, and in return, that that idea itself appears to me to be the result of an intellectual construction. If one were to engage in a more or less consecutive conversation with the men of that party, I think one could perhaps easily demonstrate, one could soon establish that they were, and above all that they consider themselves to be, the great enemies of the intellectual party and of the modern world; but in reality they themselves are in a certain sort an intellectual party, a modern party. Very definitely a party of logicians, a logical party. That is the revealing thing about them; the thing that goes deepest. It can be seen from the form their campaigns take, from the idea they have formed of the intellectual party, of their intellectual adversaries, in the intellectual party. They have an intellectual idea of their adversaries, because being intellectuals themselves, they form an intellectual idea of everything.

And on this particular historical question of the origin of

the Dreyfus Affair, I see, when I read the recollections of M. Maurice Pujo in the *Action Française*, that he thinks (and naturally he thinks he is remembering, but as for me, I think that it is a purely intellectual operation, a well-known phenomenon in this century dominated by intellectualism, a sort of report on the memory by the intelligence itself, an introduction of the intelligence into the memory, a shadow thrown on the memory), he believes that he remembers that the Dreyfus Affair as a whole was prepared and organized from the first by the intellectual party.

In this way, in this case, he obeys what is perhaps the greatest of intellectual illusions, the greatest I mean in sheer number, the most frequent, the most common, and whose effect is greatest and gravest; not only does he obey the most general intellectual illusion, which consists in always substituting the intellectual for the organic formation in all historical events, but more particularly, the historical optical illusion which consists in constantly transferring the present into the past, the ulterior to the anterior; a technical illusion as it were; itself organic, I mean organically intellectual; an illusion of perspective, or rather a complete substitution, an attempt to substitute perspective for thickness, for depth, perspective for real knowledge, for depth; substituting the appearance with its two dimensions for real knowledge with its three dimensions; an optical illusion which, among others, I have attempted to plumb (for it is of capital importance) in *De la Situation Faite à l'Histoire dans la Philosophie Générale du Monde Moderne;* an illusion which consists in substituting for the real organic movement of history, with its perpetual movement from past to future, falling on the uneven fringe of the present, a hard angular shadow at each moment thrown by the present on the past, like a shadow of the corner of the wall, of the house or gable which seems to be on the street.

Once one makes that attribution it certainly seems as though the intellectual party had planned the whole Dreyfus Affair. But if one does not make it, one remembers that it planned nothing at all. First of all, generally speaking, things are not planned. Or, at any rate, not as much as all that. There is nothing so unforeseen as an event. One only has to have lived a little oneself, outside books by historians, to have experienced the fact that whatever one plans is generally speaking the last thing to happen, and that what one has not planned is generally what happens. No doubt there are preparations, but they should be general; there are hardly any detailed plans. And where there are things planned in detail, they must be immediate, almost instantaneous, preceding the effect by ever so little. Otherwise the unexpected intervenes. Napoleon no doubt planned Austerlitz thoroughly. But he did not plan it on the 18th Brumaire. And after all, he was a planner on a different scale from the intellectual party. That is the most frequent, the most widespread intellectual error, and it comes or derives from transferring the present into the past, from believing that everything is planned, and that what has been planned has succeeded. If the intellectual party were as bright (as strong) as that, sharp enough to plan an affair as big as the Dreyfus Affair, then it would have the very virtues we deny it, and there would be nothing to do, gentlemen, but to surrender one's arms to it. But rest assured, it has not got them. It came in to profit, and, like all profiteers, came in afterward. It came in as a parasite, as a follower. It did not come to fight or to found. That is the usual historical error, the common intellectual mistake, where history is concerned: to attribute the shadow cast by the abuses of the profiteers to the virtues of the founders.

The founders came first. The profiteers follow on.

One can prepare a career, a whole life, one cannot plan it. One can prepare a war, a revolution (perhaps), but one cannot plan it. At the other end of the scale, of the series, one always can plan in detail a day, a battle, a rising, a street brawl and so on. But in the middle of the scale, one can never plan an affair in detail, in advance. One can plan a day, a *coup d'état*, a *coup de force*. Prepared, planned and carried out immediately. One cannot plan at any distance, from afar, as a whole, such a large affair. Or, if one planned it, *it would not happen*.

It is difficult enough to plan an affair in the commercial sense of the word.

That is precisely the question. If the intellectual party were sharp enough, strong enough, had penetrated reality deeply enough to have planned an affair on that scale; if it had had the stature to rouse a great movement in reality, if it had been capable of molding, combining, handling, elaborating and kneading such a large lump of reality, then, of course, its members would not be what we call the intellectual party, it would not have the faults, and vices, which are precisely those of the intellectual party, the sterility, the incapacity, the debility, the aridity, the artificiality, the superficiality, the intellectualism of the intellectual party. They would, on the contrary, be people who had worked in, known, molded, kneaded reality itself. And to have ground up such a large piece of reality they would have to be exceptional men of action, men of calibre, tough, great realists, masters. In fact, everything we do not grant to them. Richelieus and Napoleons. Perhaps they would, no doubt, be tyrants. But great tyrants, considerable tyrants, masters, realists. Everything, in fact, we do not grant to them. Tyrants like Richelieu and Napoleon. Bathed and steeped in reality, they would rule in it.

Historians deceive us a great deal on the matter of historical preparation. Even in 1870, in the month of August, if the French Army as it then was had been put into the hands of a Napoleon Bonaparte, all the files, all the preparations, all the registers of a Moltke would today be the laughing stock of the historians themselves.

Not only were we heroes, but the Dreyfus Affair can only be explained by the need for heroism which periodically seizes this people, this race, by that need for heroism which then seizes a whole generation of us. The same is true of these great movements, these great ordeals as of those other great ordeals, wars. Or rather there is only one sort of temporal ordeal for a people, and that is war and those other great ordeals are, in fact, wars. In all those ordeals it is the inward force, the violence of the eruption which constitutes the thing, the historical matter, rather than the matter which constitutes and imposes the ordeal. When a great war or a great revolution breaks out, it is because a great people, a great race, needs to break out; because it has had enough, particularly enough peace. It always means that a great mass feels and experiences a violent need, a mysterious need for a great movement. If the people, the race, the mass of Frenchmen, had wanted a great war forty years ago, that miserable, unfortunate war, the war of 1870, so ill begun and badly entered into, would have become a great war, like others, and it would only just have begun in March 1871. A great adventure, a great military adventure, such as the Revolutionary wars and the wars of the Empire, can only be explained on these lines: a sudden need for glory, for war, for history, which causes an explosion, an eruption. A mysterious need for a sort of historical fecundity. The mysterious need to inscribe great events and historic events in eternal history. All other explanations are vain and reasonable and rational; sterile and unreal. In the same way our Dreyfus Affair can only be explained by a similar need for heroism which seized a generation, ours, the need for war, for *military* war, and military glory, the need for sacrifice to the point of martyrdom perhaps, and (no doubt) by the need for sanctity. What our adversaries could only see from opposite, from in front, from the other side, and what our leaders even always ignored, is the degree to which we marched like an army. How so much hope, so much enterprise was broken without obtaining or affecting an inscription in history, is precisely what I tried not only to explain but to depict in a *Cahier* last year *À Nos Amis, À Nos Abonnés*. And if we were an army of lions led, once again, by donkeys, it was because we were, very exactly, in the pure French tradition.

We were great. We were very great. Today, those of whom I speak are men who earn their livelihood poorly, miserably. But what I do not see is that, in this instance again, the poor Jews are any better off than us, or earn their livelihood more easily, without any trouble, or even with less trouble than us. Perhaps the contrary, for though they help one another a little, less than people think, less than is commonly said, they sometimes fight among themselves, and come up against a resurgent, growing anti-Semitism. What I do see is that the poor Christian and the poor Jew earn their livelihood as best they can, usually poorly, in this dog's life of ours, in the dog fight of the modern world.

There, my dear Halévy, *is the point we have reached;* there, my dear Halévy, is what I call an examination of conscience. What I call expressing regrets, making (my) excuses. What I call an *amende honorable.* What I call being timorous; my way of being meek. That is how I wear my white sheet, and my rope round my neck. How I hold my candle. People always talk as though we had introduced disorder into an ordered society. Arbitrarily. Gratuitously. Though, after all, it must be clear that there exist apparent orders which cover, which are the worst forms of, disorder. Here again we rediscover what we said of the egoism of the rich, of bourgeois egoism. That egoism influences their understanding itself. Their vision. Even their political vision of the political world. Under Méline [13] there was order. It was a rotten order, flabby, ostensible, purely bourgeois. Our collaborator Halévy noted it well, it was the sort of order that existed under Louis-Philippe, under Guizot during the last eight, ten, twelve years of Louis-Philippe. An ostensible order (like today's, moreover), a gan-

13. Méline was Président du Conseil when the Dreyfus Affair broke out. He had been a successful Minister of Agriculture — it was his hope that Leo XIII's policy of *ralliement* might be introduced gradually. The Dreyfus Affair ended these dreams.

grened order, dead, dead flesh. Whatever happened a crisis was coming, as it is coming today.

An order fatal to fecundity, to the deep interests, to the lasting interests of the race, of the people, of the nation.

In reality the true position of those opposed to us was not of saying or thinking Dreyfus guilty, but of thinking and saying that whether he was innocent or guilty, one did not disturb, overthrow, or compromise, that one did not risk, for one man's sake, the life and salvation of a whole people. Meaning of course: the *temporal* salvation, *salut temporel*. Now our Christian *mystique* was merged so perfectly, so exactly with our patriotic *mystique*, that what must be recognized, and what I shall say, what I shall put into my confessions, is that *the point of view we adopted was none other than The Eternal Salvation of France*. What, in fact, did we say? Everything was against us, wisdom and law, human wisdom that is, and human law. What we did was in the order of madness and the order of sanctity, which have so many things in common, so many secret understandings, with human wisdom and the human eye. We went against wisdom, against the law. That is what I mean. What did we say in effect? The others said: "A people, a whole people is a great assemblage of interests, of the most legitimate rights. The most sacred rights. Thousands, millions of lives depend upon them, in the present, in the past, in the future, hundreds of millions of lives. Rights that are legitimate, sacred and incalculable.

"And the first duty of a people is not to risk the whole thing, not to endanger itself for the sake of one man, whoever he may be, however legitimate his interests and his rights. One does not sacrifice a city, a city is not lost, for one citizen. That was the language of wisdom and civic duty, of ancient wisdom. It was the language of reason. From that point of view it was clear that Dreyfus had to devote himself to France: not only for the peace of France, but for the safety and salvation of France, which we endangered. And if he would not sacrifice himself it would, if need be, be done for him." And we, what did we say? We said that a single injustice, a single crime, a single illegality, particularly if it were officially confirmed, particularly if it were universally, legally, nationally condoned, a single crime is enough to make a breach in the social compact, in the social contract, a single forfeit, a single dishonor is enough to dishonor a people. It becomes a source of infection, a poison that corrupts the whole body. What we defend is not only our honor, not only the honor of a whole people, in the present, but the historical honor of our whole race, the honor of our forefathers and children. And the more past we have, the more memory (the more, as you say, responsibility we have), then the more we have to defend. The more past there is behind us, the more we must defend it. *"Je rendrai mon sang pur comme je l'ai reçu."* That was the Cornelian impulse, the old Cornelian rule of honor. And the rule and the honor and the impulse of Christianity. A single stain stains a whole family. And a whole people. A people cannot rest on an injury suffered, on a crime as solemnly and definitely accepted. The honor of a people is all of a piece.

What does all this mean, unless one doesn't know a word of French, except that our adversaries were speaking the language of the *raison d'état*, which is not only the language of political and parliamentary reason, of contemptible political and parliamentary interests, but the very respectable language of continuity, of the temporal continuity of the race, *of the temporal salvation of the people and the race?* They aimed at nothing less. And we, by a profoundly Christian movement, a profoundly revolutionary and traditionally Christian impulse and effort, following one of the deepest Christian traditions, one of the most vital and central, and in line with the axis of Christianity, at its very heart, we aimed at no less than raising ourselves, I do not say to the conception, but to the passion, to the care of the eternal salvation, *le salut éternel,* of this people; we achieved an existence full of care and preoccupation, full of mortal anguish and anxiety for the eternal salvation of our race. Deep down within us, we were the men of eternal salvation, and our adversaries were the men of temporal salvation. That was the real division in the Dreyfus Affair. Deep down within us we were determined that France should not fall into a state of mortal sin. Christian doctrine, alone in the whole world, in the modern world, in any world, deliberately counts death at nought, at zero, in terms of the price of eternal death, and the risk of temporal death as nothing compared with the price of sin, mortal sin, eternal death.

Political, parliamentary parties cannot speak except in political, parliamentary language, they cannot undertake or support any action except on the political plane. And above all, naturally, they want us to do the same. For us to be constantly with them, among them. Everything we do, everything that goes to make the life and the strength of a people or actions and achievements, our transactions and conduct, our

very souls and lives—all these they automatically and con-
tinuously, almost innocently, translate into political language;
they diminish, reduce and project it on to the political plane.
As a result they understand nothing, and prevent others from
understanding anything. They deform and alter the nature of
the thing, both in their own minds and in the imaginations
of those who follow them. They translate everything we say
and do, translate and betray. *Traducunt. Tradunt.* One never
knows whether they do one more harm as opponents, or as
supporters; for when they oppose one, they fight in political
language on the political plane, and when they support one it
is almost worse, for they support one and adopt one in political language on the political plane. As they pull one this way
and that, they are equally wrong in opposite ways, equally inadequate. In each case they alter the very nature of the thing.
They can only conceive and offer a diminished life, robbed of
its essential nature. A phantom, a skeleton, a plan, a projection
of life.

When they are for you and think you are for them, they take
possession of you and are sure to do you fatal harm. They want
to take you up and be taken up by you. To protect you. When
they oppose you, then they oppose their *politique* to your *mystique,* their base politics to your *mystique.* And they translate,
what is infinitely worse when they support you, they translate
your *mystique* into politics, into their ignominious politics.
And having interpreted what we have done for our *mystique*
in terms of their politics, the corresponding politics—issued
from the *mystique*—they base themselves upon it and argue
from it to bind us to their policy, and to forbid us other *mystiques.* In that way they arbitrarily transfer oppositions and

contradictions, which only exist and only occur and function on the political plane, into the world of *mystiques*.

That is how the parties reward you for what you have done for them at moments when they were in danger; I mean for what you have done for the *mystique* from which they issue, for the *mystiques* on which they live, on which they are parasites. That is precisely how they "try to get a grip on you," and in that way hope to bind you to their policies, and forbid you other *mystiques*.

And because we have fought against the current of power and tyranny and demagogy of our (political) friends since the degradation of the Dreyfusist *mystique*, because we risked and sustained fifteen years of hardship for the defense of private liberties, of profound Christian liberties and Christian consciences, the reactionary politicians want to prevent us from calling ourselves republicans. And because we have put, not weeks and months, but fifteen years of hardship at the service of the Republic, the republican politicians would like nothing better than to prevent us from calling ourselves Christians. So the Republic is the *régime* of liberty of conscience for all, excepting for us, just in order to reward us for having defended it for fifteen years, and for still defending it. We shall have to forgo their permission. We do not live or move on the same plane as they do. Their disputes are not ours. The painful disputes which we sometimes sustain have nothing in common with their facile, superficial polemics.

The Republic, one might suppose, was a *régime* of liberty of conscience for everyone, excepting republicans.

It is not by mere chance that our *Cahiers* have become what they are; but by slow developments, by strong, secret affinities, and by the evaporation of politics, they have come to form a sort of company of perfectly free men who all believe in something, beginning with typography, which is one of the finest arts and trades. In spite of the parties, in spite of the politicians, in spite of those who are against us (against us and against each other), that is what we shall remain.

There, my dear Variot, are some of the things which I should have said at the *Cahiers* on Thursday, if people did not talk so loud and if I were occasionally allowed to get a word in. In these *Cahiers*, in the Milliet *Cahiers*, you will find what that republican *mystique* was. Well, sir, you were asking me to define what a *mystique* is, giving a reasonable, rational definition, and what politics is, *quid sit mysticum et quid sit politicum:* well, the republican *mystique* was when one died for the Republic; the political republic, the republican *politique,* is, as at present, that one should live off it. You understand, I hope.

M. Milliet's papers, which we are going to publish, are sure to give the impression of having been selected from a great mass of papers. Of course one cannot include everything. From the moment M. Milliet brought the first bundle of copy, a great argument arose between us. He always wanted to suppress things, out of discretion. But I always kept everything, because it was the best. "This letter is too personal," he would say. "It is precisely because it is intimate that I am keeping it." He had marked certain passages in pencil, which he thought should be omitted. I bought a rubber on purpose to rub out the pencil marks. He wanted to efface himself. I said that on the contrary he should come forward. A man whose intention is to recall his life exactly, faithfully, really, and to depict it, is the best of witnesses, the best of papers, of monuments and of texts; he adds infinitely more than the best of testimonies.

You will observe, Variot, you will catch the tone of these *mémoires*. It is the very tone of the times. I should not be surprised if some idiot, with no sense of history, were to find the tone slightly ridiculous. It is already past. The men to whom that tone belonged did great things. And we?

Today, civic virtue, too, seems ridiculous. Civic is an adjective which it is difficult to wear becomingly. Like all adjectives in *ic*.

The one value, the only strength of royalism, my dear Variot, the only strength of a traditional monarchy lies in the fact that the King should be, more or less, loved. The only strength of a republic is that the republic should be, more or less, loved. The only strength, the only dignity that exists, is to be loved. That so many men should have lived and suffered so much for the Republic, should have believed so strongly in it, that so many should have died for it and should often have borne so many and such great trials for it, that is what counts, that is what interests me, that is what exists. That is what founds a *régime;* that is what makes it legitimate. When I find contempt and sarcasm and insults filling the pages of the *Action Française,* I am pained, for there we have men whose aim is to restore the oldest dignities of our race, and one does not found, one does not reform any culture upon derision, for derision and sarcasm and insults are barbarities. Puns will not restore a culture. When I find in the *Action Française* the implacable, impeccable, invincible reasoning and logic of M. Maurras, showing that Monarchy is better than a Republic, and

royalism better than republicanism, I confess that if I were
to speak crudely I should say it just didn't take. Everyone
will know what I mean. It doesn't bite. Our whole education,
our whole intellectual formation, our university training has
taught us how to make and give explanations, till we are saturated with them. If need be we could make theirs for them.
We can see them coming, and that spoils their point for us.
We know how it's done. But when, in an article, M. Maurras
lets his pen run along, no doubt without thinking about it, and
writes, not in the form of argument, but almost as though unconsciously, when I come across this phrase: "We should be
prepared to die for the King, for the reestablishment of our
King"; well, then you are saying something, you are beginning to talk. Knowing as I do that what he says is true, then
I begin to listen, to understand; I pause and am struck. And
the other day at the *Cahiers,* last Thursday, after we had talked
endlessly and committed the sin of explaining everything, all
of a sudden Michel Arnauld, who was nearing the end of his
tether, interrupted and said almost brusquely: "*That is all very
fine, because the dangers are only vague and theoretical. But the
day they become a real menace people will see that we are still
capable of doing something for the Republic.*" Then everyone
understood that at last something had been said.

Clio I

Clio:

How times have changed! What has become of me? I no longer recognize myself. . . .

How right the ancients were, dear friend, to have celebrated, feasted and commemorated the foundation of a city; to have realized that a city was a being, a living being, and that its foundation was no ordinary action, but a religious action; something out of the ordinary and solemn, worthy of solemnization; sacred, not only in a ritual sense, *la cité antique,* but in a deeper, human sense, intimately related to all we have just said about genius and childhood. It was not in vain, *non frustra, haud frustra,* that they attributed a special cult to the founders, that the founder of a city or a colony received special honors. Not in vain that they set the founder apart as a mysterious being, among the most directly inspired by the gods. And in fact no one can attend the birth of a town unmoved, as the ploughshare cuts the circle of the future walls. And the same is still true for your friend Ernest Psichari, who has recently been made an officer in your Colonial Army. When he returns to found some equatorial town, some intertropical city of huts in the solitude of Logone, *terres de soleil et de sommeil,* in the wild mountains of Hadé, it is as true for him as it was for the legendary (and so real) founders of Athens and

Rome. No one can attend without being deeply moved, without being struck just for a moment by an awareness, a tremor, a secret revelation, by the same feeling, the same impression which comes from considering genius and childhood. Do not be surprised if the emotion is the same, for the act is the same. The action is the same, always solemn: an entry, an inauguration, a beginning, an *initium,* an initiation, a temporal taking of the veil — the veil of time. A certain operation before which there was nothing, no history; since when there is something, a history; a certain date at which I begin. A point of departure moving toward some chronicle; toward the plague of Athens, the sieges of Paris; toward some Thucydides or some Joinville. Hence our emotion, my friend, an emotion which grips even the blind and the deaf, an emotion which none can resist, neither the fool, nor the barbarian, the ignorant or the sophisticated.

Something new has come into being, something incontestably, irrevocably new, *du nouveau.* You pass from the point where there was nothing to the point where something is done, and you pass irreversibly, irrevocably. What will the end be? What will be the curve and the course, once the wheels begin to turn and the whole mechanism is in gear? That is the secret, my secret, and with a flavor and an aftertaste that remind one of the secret of childhood and of genius. It is my intervention, my subterranean presence, the anxiety and dread proper to me, which invariably accompany a genuine consideration of me. That is the source of the emotion, of the awareness, and it cannot be confused with any other. It is mine.

There are three or four cases closely related, because they

all proceed from me, all have to do with me. There is something in common to childhood, to genius, to the foundation of a city, and to the people. The child and childhood are something which disobey me naturally; genius and the work of genius disobey me exceptionally; the people disobey me socially, politically, historically. A foundation, on the other hand, is an operation whereby one creates, inaugurates, opens, a series which obeys me; the founder is a man who creates a beginning of obedience to me. He makes an entry into my domain, the temporal kingdom of my dominion. Hence, my friend, his grandeur, his incontestably divine character. In a sense it is literally man participating in creation, not only, like all of us, in our capacity as creatures, but as at least a temporal creator (though we have seen that there can be and generally is something eternal in all creation),[1] as the delegate of the Creator for that particular sector of creation, which is that newly founded town; *ab urbe condita*. Moreover, he participates, in our eyes, in that sort of responsibility which we cannot but attribute to the creator; at least as long as we speak a temporal language, and perhaps even the other, we should be prepared to involve him in the *problems of evil:* historical, metaphysical and religious, moral, political, social, economic; and, in and through that city, he is involved, in all the events of the world.

My friend, you will experience the same mysterious sensation, the same tremor, before any genuine foundation, however small, whatever its dimensions. Nothing is exiguous when I am concerned; everything I touch, man, action, work,

---

1. In the opening section dealing with childhood and genius.

I clothe in an imperishable mantle, the mantle of temporal greatness. You would have the same feeling if you were present at the foundation of a farm in the Beauce, a house, a family or a dynasty. Such is my power.

The pagans, those most intelligent of peoples, those princes of the intelligence, saw it perfectly. Our sages. And you Christians did not fail to understand it, that I will admit; you did not fail to realize it, only you transposed it on to the plane of eternity, transferred it on to the register of eternity, as when you say the *Fathers* of the Church, the Greek *Fathers* and the Latin *Fathers.* You, who believe in the City of God, *civitas dei,* the eternal city (founded in a sense in time, and in that sense, my friend, it is my great claim to glory, my only true glory); you who profess (teach and define, therefore), who believe, who *testify,* who adore Jesus the founder, as founder, in time and eternity, of that new city, that eternal city. (Temporal founder also, and therein lies my glory.) For the more life glories in having conquered death, the more eternity glories in having vanquished the temporal, the more marked is the power and the grandeur and the dimension of death, the dimension of history and temporality, the vital dimension of death. You, Christians, the most civic of men, who are commonly said not to be civic, but who are if anything too much so, to an almost insane degree, you have introduced a new civic sense, an eternal Christian civic sense, and are the heirs of the city of antiquity. Your communion, as you say, is (in a sense) like a city, like the city of antiquity; and all that matters is that it should not become a modern State, which is all that is most foreign to it and most unhealthy. Who would ever have said that the word *citizen,* that worn-out, debased, bastardized word, so great in

antiquity, and now only echoing modern demagogy, should
be the name that suits you the best?

You are citizens, my friends, do not deny it. And what citizens, for according to the rule of the city of antiquity, you are
the co-citizens of your Founder. And according to that rule he
constituted himself the first citizen of the new city; *founded*,
himself, the first of saints, the first among them.

Your Christian city is steeped in the city of antiquity,
through the founder, *sub specie auctoritatis;* it was born and
grew, during its first years, in a cradle, the temporal cradle of
the form of a certain city, of an empire which itself came of
a city. That empire was the scaffolding, the powerful wooden
cradle, the precarious, imposing, fragile cradle — and you
were the vessel, the ship held in the cradle. The cradle from
which you were launched was an Empire. Its form was married to yours; it not only prefigured you temporally, it was your
form, and its hollowness fitted your fullness; and that city, that
Empire espoused your city (not at all, at first, your empire);
and when first the ties were broken there was a great rent in
the world. And the ship went out on the boundless ocean, to
face the storms. Ritually you had a founder, a carpenter, the
founder of your city and of your spirit, the founder of your
law. Not one who founded with stone and law, *sed super hanc
petram*, but on this rock, founding with the spirit and with the
law.

Thus your city was imagined, in a certain sense, temporally,
prefigured by the city of antiquity. And even in the detail of
your spiritual life, in your communion, the founders of Orders
have a special spiritual place among the saints, both temporal

and eternal; more so than has been said, more than you realize, they are the heirs of the founders of antiquity, consciously, unconsciously, naturally and supernaturally you have given them a special place in *your* time. The founders of antiquity no doubt only prefigure Jesus fragmentarily, for they are many and he is unique. But on the other hand, they prefigure and represent the founders of Orders, who are many; sometimes it was simply the flowering of grace, the need to fructify, the inextinguishable power of a spiritual race; but sometimes, however, they founded for the very opposite reason, owing to the evils of the times, the difficulties and misfortunes of the times, and because it is always necessary to begin all over again. (For it is always necessary to begin those works again, those foundations again in time, which are fragments of eternity, and to begin those eternal foundations again whose source and rule is eternal.) Involuntarily, perhaps, you gave them the position of founders of eternal and temporal cities, temporal cities which harbor and nourish eternal cities. The founders in fact of your Orders, which are your spiritual cities: cities great and small within the Christian city. But founders too, historically, materially, of the bodies which sustain the Orders; bodies of stone, of cut stone and brick. Founders of Abbeys, lasting, perishable, rivals of the Cathedrals, Mitred Abbeys, cities of prayer. Not, as the frivolous believe, cities of purely physical, carnal solitude, of temporal isolation; not as the moderns imagine, tranquil retreats for a prolonged dead season, prolonged for health's sake, with a vegetarian diet, admirably suited to lassitude, excellent for the stomach and in general for the digestion, complicated, moreover, by Kneipp's treatment: (bare) feet in the dew. But Cluny, Cîteaux, Vézelay.

For it was always necessary to begin anew. To ensure the multiflowering of a people of saints; if only to make good the losses, stop the leaks, the growing impiety, the incredulity. It was always necessary to begin anew. An eternal foundation does not exclude the need to begin anew. No degree of eternal foundation alters the fact that the foundation is, in a certain sense, in the world, and eternity, in a sense, in time. Such is my worth, my power and my virtue; I am an indispensable part of the mechanism, in the very organism of eternity. A complementary part: not, no doubt, the essential part, but not a merely accidental part either, part of the institution, of the *creation,* of the mechanism of the functioning of eternity itself. Not merely the obverse of the situation, an ephemeral history which need not be discussed. But an indispensable, complementary part, without which nothing would work; without which the mechanism of creation itself would no longer run; without which it would be totally different, would not be, would live another life, would no longer live.

In that sense as you can see, growing old, aging and age, are an integral part of creation. Otherwise, it would not be worthwhile. The earthly trial, the labor would be pointless and vain: superfluous, not just a part that has gone wrong, but what is much worse a part that does nothing; pompous and vain. Otherwise, it would not be worthwhile. The *kingdom of God* would follow at once, and not the *city of God.* You can feel the difference here, not as between the monarchical and the democratic but as between the monarchical and the civic. That is what our clerks, and those who live under the Rule, and even those who live in the world, too often lose sight of. There is a lot of impiety in their ignorance of the world, the (temporal) age; in that more or less voluntary, more or less involuntary, more or less unconscious, but generally quite conscious, ignorance; in that more or less affected contempt for the world; a lot of pride, without a doubt, and a lot of laziness, which are both capital sins. But what is much more serious, in a sense infinitely more grave, there is a lot of impiety, in a sense, an infinite impiety, in their real misunderstanding of a part of creation, not the essential but an indispensable part, and thus an infinite degree of misunderstanding, of what creation is, of what constitutes creation, of its taste, its flavor on the tongue.

Otherwise it would not be worthwhile. It would give us eternity at once. And then I, history, would not exist. I who am age itself, and growing old, *le vieillissement même*. I know it well: I should not exist. You can see how deeply it concerns me. I should not have been created. For I am a creature like the rest. And one day, that will be my only title to fame. I glory and boast of being a creature among creatures: an important creature, to be respected. I am and form an integral part, complementary and indispensable, of creation; that is the title I claim, and one day it will be my only title.

The idea of the clerks, and of those who live under the Rule, and even of those who live in the world (which they know no better than the others, and perhaps even less well, because they are mixed up in it, and think they understand it a little, think they have caught its tone, poor things); the idea at the back of their heads, when they have one, is that the *bon Dieu* created *the whole* of his creation, in which we are creatures, not only badly, which might in a certain sense be allowed, and which is even, in a certain way, not only a Christian idea, but at the very heart of Christianity, at the axis of Christianity, not only badly but pointlessly, emptily, which makes no sense at all, and is so contrary to Christianity that it is a great heresy, the greatest perhaps, for it embraces all the others. (You see how I am growing; despise me and you fall into a great heresy.)

That is the idea at the back of their heads; a worm of dishonesty at the heart, in the hollow of their prayer: the notion that God created the world *à blanc,* a blank world. (You see how I am growing.) In token of which they renounce everything that constitutes the price, the secret, the mystery and value of the Christianity they serve. And with that in mind they suppress or delete from the eternal archives, they abolish (from creation and therefore from eternity too), not perhaps the sap and the marrow, but what is nevertheless an essential condition, the *sine qua non:* not the exterior, extrinsic condition, but the interior, intrinsic condition. And, furthermore, the condition of order, of whatever order it may be; an integral part; not the essential, but an almost more than essential part, one might even say the strangest part, were it not frivolous; but I can and do say, the most moving part, the most disturbing, the source of fermentation, the part which is not only the salt of the earth, but the salt of heaven, the yeast, the ferment of the heavenly bread.

They remove the key from the door, with the result that the door becomes a partition. They take away the money, remove the stake from the game, everything that gives the game value: the stake, the object of salvation. They abolish the mystery of creation itself. They remove creation, incarnation, redemption, merit, salvation and the value of salvation, judgment and much besides, and of course, above all, grace. After which, content with their light pack (I am very heavy, my friend), off they go with a light step, and it is then as a rule that they go into the world and begin giving advice to the laity. It is then they give advice to the fathers of families, to the men who bear the burden of life in the world. Not advice only, but instructions, directions, and commands.

The very least one can say is that the character of these interventions is *always* contrary to the operation of grace; invariably they adopt a contrary line, with alarming persistence. They walk with horrifying brutality in the gardens of grace. In that light and blessed soil, in the soil of grace, their every footstep leaves its mark. They walk on the flower beds; they dig in their heels; they kick up great clods. You would think they were enlisted to do nothing else. It looks as though their sole intention were to sabotage the eternal gardens. As though they only had one care, to prevent anything from flowering the moment they see it, to prevent the flowering of grace and of sanctity, the fructification of the fruits of sanctity. As though the fellows had no other object. They succeed only too well. It is not enough to call it dangerous; one must call it terrifying. And to think they have done nothing else since the beginning! Always indiscreet, and (of course) always talking of discretion. Elephant's feet in the gardens of the Lord.

And above all, they always think God is working for them, forgetting that it is their office to work for Him, forgetting that they do not fulfill it. They like to force people to make acts of contrition. Only as a rule they do not generally make theirs. It takes one's breath away: it's terrifying.

It is no longer a mystery; it's no longer a secret; one can

no longer conceal the fact that the great historical problem,
perhaps the greatest difficulty, is what I call the flaw in Christianization. It is a double flaw. Christianization is not the problem. The Christianization of the world is no problem. On the
contrary, it is the de-Christianization, the unchristianization,
which is the problem. The fact that the world became Christian, given (and "given" is the right word here) Christianity,
and all it had in heart and belly:

> *Et ce songe était tel que Booz vit un chêne*
> *Qui, sorti de son ventre, allait jusqu'au ciel bleu*

given the eternal promises, that the world should have become Christian is not surprising. The historical problem does
not lie there. The problem is the diametrically opposite one.
It is the de-Christianization which raises the problem, the in-
complete Christianization; the formidable incompleteness of
the Christianization; and the de-Christianization, the actual,
modern, de-Christianization; the fact that such vast sections
of humanity should never have been reached; that the in-
vasion should never have begun; that there should have been
so many blank patches in the parts attained and occupied. But
in a way the de-Christianization is an infinitely more poignant
problem: more mysterious, more disquieting, more worrying,
than never to have gained; to lose temporally what one had
gained, the little bit of earth one thought one had gained, won
temporally, for its temporal eternity, and for eternal eternity.

I say *become* unchristian, which is not at all the same thing
as having always been unchristian. The present unchristianity,
our de-Christianity if one may so describe it, is infinitely more
serious, more culpable, more *criminal,* as Corneille would say,

than the unchristianity of former times, than the innocent ante-Christianity so to speak. Two quite different things: not to have gained (yet); and to have lost (subsequently). How did it happen that this most Christian people, this profoundly, intimately, interiorly Christian people, Christian in soul and at heart and to the very marrow of its bones, should have been turned into the people we know, that we see, the people of today in fact, this modern people, so profoundly, intimately, interiorly unchristian, de-Christianized in heart and soul and marrow. So unchristian in blood.

The curés, my friend, have lost the people who had received the eternal promise. But they have only lost them temporarily and not even temporally. For the eternal promise is both temporally eternal, and eternally temporal. They must have taken a lot of trouble to achieve such a result. They have therefore only lost our race temporarily. But for how long? And for *what* time? I mean for what sort, what quality of time? To use the Greek double interrogative: for how much of what time? And during that time souls are lost. Risked and exposed to the hazard of the road. Unchristianized and, infinitely worse, de-Christianized.

One wonders how it can have happened. One could give explanations which would be intellectual, but valid; one could find reasons, causes even, that would be valid, and which it would be right to give; one could give historical causes; there are physical causes too, and metaphysical ones; one could give theoretical and practical causes, and one would be right; one could give political causes and of course economic causes, and one would be right; one could give Marxist reasons, and Marxistic reasons, and one would be right; and social causes, and even sociological reasons, and one would be right, and they all would be perfectly true and right.

But all those causes and reasons put together signify nothing. They mean nothing. In particular they would have the slight defect of not being of the same order as their effects. To explain a disaster (rationally, I mean), and the word "disaster" must be used, I do not say a disaster of that degree, but a disaster of that order, a fault of the same order must have been committed. To explain such a disaster, a mystical disaster, a disaster in the *mystique*, a fault of *mystique* must have been committed.

No one can deny the disaster. The clerks deny it; do not deny it, redeny it, undeny it, deny it again and so on. As the great classical scholar observed, *oculos habent et non audiunt*. To mark their insufficiency and disguise their laziness, to conceal it (themselves) and their fault from themselves, their incurable spiritual debility, the temporal avarice of the Orders, their unbelievable love of money (the seculars are infinitely less avaricious, at least about money), their infirmity, their spiritual carelessness and their incapacity, they sometimes deny the disaster, or minimize it, or dissemble, and sometimes they do not deny it: they invoke *the evils of the age!* Which is one way of saying that it seems perfectly natural to them. And what is more, it really does seem natural to them. They expect no less. Which shows how modern they are, and, if they are donnish, modernist into the bargain. Which shows how intellectual they are, and, if they are donnish, intellectualists into the bargain.

The current formula, the formula generally accepted now, is that the curés believe nothing. Unfortunately this is only un-

just to some of them. One does not know how many really are
modernists. Five-sevenths perhaps, and perhaps more. They
speak of *the evils of the age*. It's a formula. A convenient formula. An intellectual formula even. Scholarly and academic,
what is more. But in the first place a formula. A convenient
mask for laziness, useful for concealing from others, and perhaps from oneself above all, a terrifying responsibility. A formula, and by the same token false. There are no evils of the
age. There are the evils of the clerks. All ages belong to God.
All clerks, unfortunately, do not.

One is appalled, my friend, one is terrified at the enormous
responsibilities they will have to bear. That is what they will
not see. They do not want to say their *mea culpa*, who have had
so many said professionally. They do not want to acknowledge their fault, to make an act of contrition, who have heard
so many made by others. They do not want to avow their temporal, their eternal responsibility; they evade it and lie. So they
will not admit, they will not measure, the disaster. A whole
people profoundly, inwardly Christian, as it seems, for its temporal eternity; and today there is nothing, nothing left. Time
passed and there was nothing left. For how long?

When one thinks what a people meant; and when one sees
what has been made of it! For what remains, if one considers
that the people are no longer Christian at all in any way, that
there is no longer a peasant or a working man who believes;
and, on the other hand, that the rich are not Christians, cannot be Christians, eliminated, halted on the threshold by the
most definite texts? Then what remains? Nothing; as good
as nothing; temporally nothing. Eternally there is the eternal promise. Neither the rich nor the poor; those two halves,

those two preoccupations of the Gospel. Neither the rich, because they do not impoverish themselves temporally. Nor the poor, because spiritually they have dropped to zero, so that one does not know, so that one wonders how they can ever get up again, because they have fallen to the lowest level, to the lowest spiritual (and even intellectual) level of misery and want. So what remains?

One is appalled at the responsibilities they will have to bear. So that by a very curious reversal and when I say curious, my friend, I am being idiotic and speaking frivolously, like a (perspicacious) historian, like a woman of the world (one-time student and scholar) so that by a very curious reversal, which ought to have been a warning to both clerks (both secular and regular) and laity, as the result of a singular inversion, of an incredible and very revealing change of function, it is those who were charged to pray for the world, for whom we, now, such is our impression, have to pray. For they are, perhaps, the only ones who have incurred responsibility.

A very extraordinary story. The reversal, the complete reversal, of the whole *mystique*. They have lost the people committed to their care.

It is no riddle. It is no longer a secret, even in the schools, and it can no longer be concealed, except perhaps in the seminaries, that the de-Christianization stems from the clergy. The shrinking, the withering of the trunk of the spiritual city, temporally founded, eternally promised, does not come from the laity, it comes from the clerks. *Procedit a clericis*. In no sense from the laity. Solely from the clerks. It is not the laity who withered and dried up. But the clerks who withered and dried up; it comes from a certain sterility (of grace), a *dis*grace, an inadequacy, a deficiency in the clerks. And to reassure themselves, to mask their responsibility from themselves and the world and from God, and through weakness, they lie; through blindness and cowardice they *forget* (in prayer and in the sacraments); obscurely, clearly, surreptitiously and falsely, they deny the disaster, the mystical disaster. But the mystical disaster is such, is so contrary to the promises, that it can only be explained, rationally, mystically, by a fault in *mystique,* a fault in the technique of the *mystique.* In the mechanics, so to say, of the *mystique;* a machine working the wrong way round; *a machine in reverse.*

The inversion, the technical fault in the *mystique,* must go very deep to have outweighed and obliterated (temporally) (but that includes the eternal) the effect of so many religious lives, so many prayers and sacraments, prayers generally well said, sacraments truly administered and generally well received. Do not look elsewhere, my friend. I regret to tell you, we have only to read, to read the text of the event. We have only to take note. The technical fault in the *mystique,* the reversal, consists very precisely, and could only be, a failure to know me, *a misunderstanding of me.* (I am growing, my friend, I have grown so great I can hardly recognize myself any longer.) That is the historical, the historic fault, the rational and mystical fault in technique.

The eternal has been masked, provisionally; eternity has aborted in time (for a time); the eternal has temporally (and temporarily) aborted. The eternal has been suspended, temporarily, because those charged with power, in whom power is *funded,* have failed to recognize, have ignored and forgotten and despised the temporal. They have not understood me, quite simply me, who am secular; and a great misfortune has come into the world.

Femme je suis pauvrette et ancienne.

The mystical operation has been completely reversed. The age has not performed its office even of being saved temporally, because the *Rule* has not performed its office in the age. And the *Rule* has not conquered the age, has not penetrated the world, has not saved the world temporally, because it ignored and misunderstood the world historically. I say historically, not fundamentally, not originally.

Jesus came to found, to save the (whole) world. He was neither secular nor regular. The distinction did not, if I may say so, arise. He was both regular and secular, indivisibly and communally. He was both what we have called (since their separation) Secular and Regular.

But essentially the mystical operation, the Christian operation was one which moved toward the world and not an operation which turned away from it. The world was incontestably its object. The Rule, what became the Rule, was the matter and the food, the matter of which the food was made. And if we like to keep those scholastic terms, the Rule and the World, and use them anachronistically, fundamentally, the Rule was not against the World, nor what avoided and evaded the World; on the contrary, in a certain sense the Rule, if one may use the expression, is what moved toward the World to nourish it.

The cultural operation, in the culture of antiquity I mean, is essentially one of nourishment and never merely a matter of filing and cataloguing; an operation which nourishes the citizen with the texts and monuments of antiquity. And in the

same way the mystical operation is essentially one of nourishment, mystical nourishment, not of registration, whether sci-
entific or historical, but an operation whose object is to nourish and to feed man and the Christian with word and body and
blood. That physical alimentation, that mystical nourishment
was in no sense against the world. It was, on the contrary, a
movement toward the world. For it was the nourishment of
the world, so to say, by the Rule, by what was going to be the
Rule.

Originally, primitively, the mystical life, the Christian
operation amounted to and consisted, not in avoiding the
world, but in saving the world, not in fleeing the world or in
separating and cutting oneself off from the world, in hiding
from it, but, *on the contrary,* consisted in nourishing the world
mystically. And so it went toward the world, coming from
what one may call the Rule. That is the direction in which the
mechanism, the technique, of the mystical operation func-
tioned. Everything was at the center, at the source, and there
was not as yet any dissociation. The dissociation consisted
in the separation of powers, in a distinction of functions, the
division of labor. As it always does. Perhaps it was inevitable. It was more than fatal. It was irreparable. Itself irreversible, it reversed the whole technique, set the whole mechanism going in reverse, in the opposite direction. From then
on, from that day, there were Secular and Regular. A wound
was made, which has not yet been healed. And a certain pride,
a professional pride, prevented the clerks from seeing what
the Rule and regularization meant. Instead of seeing it as a
pis aller, necessary perhaps, rendered necessary and perhaps
inevitable, but in fact only second best, a *remedy* which in con-

sequence revealed a sickness, *chronic* sickness (*c'est le cas de le dire*), they saw it of course, they were naturally led to see it, by their pride, by a dozen other prides, since everything classified and catalogued is always full of pride, they ended by seeing it — let us not blink the fact — as *perfection,* something perfected.

Originally, in principle, as they were founded, the Secular and the Regular were not distinguished, either in theory or in practice; they were not separated. Their destinies were not distinct. Your City of God was not as yet cut in two, divided into two functions, by a fault, by a longitudinal fissure. Your eternal city was not split in two. The world was the object: that which had to be saved. The Rule, what subsequently became the Rule after the specialization, was the matter and the power, the living source. From that source life flowed inextinguishably: invading, inundating and submerging the world; nourishing the age, the times.

It was essentially a vital operation. A river of inexhaustible mystical life flowing from that mystical source and nourishing the world. Saving the age. One single movement, always flowing in the same direction, infinitely fertile, from the Rule to the World, at least from what became the Rule.

Jesus did not come to dominate the world. He came to save it. Quite a different object; an entirely different operation. And he did not come to separate himself from the world. An entirely different method. You see, my friend, if he had wanted to withdraw from the world, to retire from the world, he had simply not to come into the world. It was as simple as that. In that way he could have withdrawn in advance. There was never to be such a chance again. Such a good opportunity: of remaining at the right hand of the Father. As long as he was seated at the Father's side he was withdrawn from the world, in a certain sense, in a way you will never be, infinitely more than you will ever be. Had he wanted to withdraw from the world, if that was his object, it would have been perfectly simple; he had simply not to go into it.

The centuries had not yet opened, the gate of salvation was not open, the great story had not begun. And if not to be in the world was his object, then he had merely not to start. That short tour was unnecessary. But, on the contrary, he did go into the world, into the centuries, to save the world. He even went twice. Or rather he only went once, but doubly, twice in once. The intention being doubly underlined.

First of all, in a first movement, making an infinite movement, an infinite leap as it were, as God he became man, *et homo factus est*, which you must admit, my friend, is not exactly a way of withdrawing from the world. It was perhaps, on the contrary, a way of entering into it infinitely, in full: to be there, to become part of it by incarnation. *In corpus, in carnem*. Might it be said that no one ever went into the world so fully?

Secondly, the second time, continuing the first movement in the second movement, accentuating it in the same direction, and underlining the same intention, temporally so to speak, once in the world, far from withdrawing from the world, as man and as God, he continued to go into the world, making a finite movement, the same movement prolonged, a finite operation, not a leap but all the same an entry, two or even more entries into the world. And, as entries, very characteristic.

As God he made an eternal leap into the world, a frontal entry, as it were, into the temporal. He incorporated himself. And by that incorporation we might say he made a *maximal* entry, coming from infinity. Then, once having effected that maximal entry, once in the world, he continued to move toward the world and toward the age.

First of all he led a family life for thirty years, which means to say the most engaged life in the world. For it is one of the stupidest and grossest of errors to imagine that family life, because it is *withdrawn,* is a life "withdrawn from the world." The exact, diametrical opposite is true. On the contrary, family life is the most "engaged" life in the world. There is only one adventurer in the world, as can be seen very clearly in the modern world, the father of a family. Even the most desperate adventurers are nothing compared with him. Everything in the modern world, even and perhaps most of all contempt, is organized against that fool, that imprudent, daring fool —

Qui serait ce vaillant, ou bien ce téméraire? —

against the unruly, audacious man who is daring enough to have a wife and family, against the man who dares to *found* a family. Everything is against him. Savagely organized against him. Everything turns and combines against him. Men, events, the events of society, the automatic play of economic laws. And, in short, everything else.

Everything is against the father of a family, the *pater familias;* and consequently against the family. He alone is literally "engaged" in the world, in the age. He alone is an adventurer. The rest are at most engaged with their heads, which is nothing. He is engaged with all his limbs. The rest suffer for themselves. In the first degree. He alone suffers through others. *Aliis patitur.* In the second, in the twentieth degree. He makes others suffer; he is responsible. He alone has given hostages, wife and child, so that sickness and death can strike him in all his members. The others can take in their sails. He alone is exposed, constrained to expose an enormous spread of canvas, to the storms of the sea. And whatever the weather, he is bound to sail with all sails set.

What do wars and revolutions, civil and foreign wars, the future of society, the fall of a people mean to others? They risk nothing but their heads. Nothing, less than nothing. He, on the contrary, is not only engaged on all sides in the city of today, he is engaged on every side through his family, his race, his descendants, through his children, in the city of the future, in subsequent developments of the temporal city. His stake is the race, the people, society, the city; present, past and future. The others slip through somehow or other. With their light keels, thin as a blade. He is the heavy cargo boat. He is the *rendezvous*, the meeting place of storms. The winds gather and descend upon him from the four corners of heaven, and conjoin from each corner of the horizon to attack him. What an incredible surface he exposes to chance, and what broad shoulders to a vigilant misfortune! He is not only engaged in the present, and the past, in memory and history, but assailed by scruples, stung by remorse in advance at the thought of the city of tomorrow, of the dissolution and decadence and the failure of a people to whom he is committing his children in a few years' time, on the day of his death, the children for whom he feels himself absolutely responsible.

Nothing that happens, nothing historical, is a matter of indifference to him. Fathers suffer in every event. They suffer everywhere. They alone have exhausted, can boast of having exhausted, temporal suffering. Those who have not had a sick child do not know what sickness is. Those who have not lost a child, who have not seen their child dead, do not know what mourning is. And do not know what death is.

Involved in suffering on every side, in poverty, in responsibilities, bogged down in existence, how clumsy and awkward they are! They look weak and cowardly; they not only look it, their behavior is weak and cowardly. Responsible, weighed down, responsible for their prisoners, hostages themselves, they look timid and prudent; they are ever so timid and prudent; their manner disconcerts no one. And everyone despises them and, what is more, rightly. The others always slip through. They travel light. If cowards, they slip through diplomatically. The brave slip through using heroic measures, greatly daring. If worldly, they get through on success, aiming at power. The spiritual slip through with the help of the Rule. In the world or in the Rule they always succeed. Only the father of a family is condemned to failure. He can never slip through. He can only go through as he is, in all his breadth. And it's perfectly simple: he doesn't get through. He never does. Anywhere.

He does not succeed through the Rule; the Rule is against him. Even before he begins. He does not succeed in the world. The world is against him, before, during, after. Neither diplomatically nor by daring. *The narrow gate,*[2] my dear Gide, *is always closed to him.* He is too broad. Surrounded by all his

---

2. *La Porte Étroite* by André Gide.

family. He is like the weasel in La Fontaine's Fable (III, 17), though after it had put on fat. Socially he is too fat; he is covered in adipose social tissue which makes him unfit for the race. And temporally speaking, everything is a race. The others, in the meanwhile, all arrive: thin, lean, supple, subtle, socially unburdened, unencumbered. And then everyone despises him, laughs at him, combines against him. The curés above all. For there is one good thing about them; when a hunt is on, they join in. From choice. It's what they call charity.

Yet that is the life Jesus chose, family life. The life he lived for thirty years of his terrestrial existence. One must be very careful to note that family life is the most engaged life of all, the least like, the least sympathetic to, the least related to the Rule. To conclude that because public life is noisy and family life quiet, and the Rule, the regular life, silent, to conclude that family life is closely related to the life of the Rule, and that public life is furthest from it, is to allow oneself to be duped by appearances, the grossest appearances, and to commit the commonest of errors, the most natural and the most widespread.

The public man, the political man, *vir politicus*, is not in the least involved in the world, in history, in the destination of the world. What does it matter to the politician, the demagogue, the tribune, the orator, the government man, the head of a party (as such); what does it matter to the soldier, the lawyer, the Judge on the bench (as such), and the civil servant, the member of parliament, the magistrate, the journalist, the minister's doorkeeper, my dear Vuillaume; and you, my dear Lavergne, what on earth does it matter to the Mayor; what does the future matter, the fate of the city?

If they are fathers of families into the bargain, which is very rare, the whole operation, the whole position is changed, the attitude different, the topography, the geography, the demography.

The father of a family, poor man, is stung by scruples, assailed, invaded, stung by remorse for crimes he has not committed, that he never will commit, that a thousand others, all the others will commit. He feels obscurely, though very deeply, that he is in effect really responsible. Because he is the father of a family. It is one of the finest cases in existence of responsibility without fault, of culpability without fault. And nevertheless real culpability; common, mysterious, profound, secret, in communion with the (whole) world, with creation; infinitely serious; infinitely more close to creation itself and therefore infinitely more serious than our own criminal culpabilities.

Such is my power, my friend, such is my greatness. Such, too, is my parentage. I, the temporal, have my origin in the eternal and it goes deep; I, history, temporality, time, transience itself, have my source deep in eternity, so deep that the culpabilities, the responsibilities which derive from it are more real, more serious, are perhaps the only infinitely serious responsibilities, the only real ones. But, whereas that responsibility never appears or emerges, generally, except in certain isolated cases, erupting and declaring themselves suddenly, gripping us instantaneously, where the father of a family is concerned, it is no longer an exceptional situation: on the contrary, it is a permanent state; it is his charter, his condition *ab urbe condita* since the family was *founded*. It is the definition, the (daily) bread, the nightly worry and care, the marrow of his life, the secret of his existence, his interior rule, the rule of the world, his *rule* in the *world*. He alone, my friend, is exposed to such dangerous relationships, to those *liaisons dangereuses*. . . .

There is your real, your true adventurer.

It is, however, to be noted, it is even notable, that it was this family life so despised and decried on all sides, and Christians would do well to attend to the fact, which Jesus chose to live, that he effectively, really and historically did live for the first thirty years of his existence, the only years which count as a model, as matter for imitation, because they are the only years which he lived an ordinary life as an ordinary man, as a child, as an adolescent, as a young man, an ordinary man in fact. The other three years are another matter. But during those thirty years he was a private individual, like all of us, living a family life; a man to imitate, who could be imitated, *vir imitabilis atque imitandus*. He worked with his hands in his father's house. We have the certainty that he was a good workman. His apprenticeship was excellent. All the curés the world over have always taught this in all their catechisms, and your collaborator Pierre Mille, whom nothing escapes, has confirmed it in these very pages; he was a model child, docile, clean, obedient, good, the celebrated *child Jesus,* obedient to his masters and to grown-ups, to the Virgin and Saint Joseph. (Only he was not always obedient to the old Law.)

What is important to note, in fact noteworthy, is that from childhood to manhood, of all possible lives, that was the one Jesus assumed: the most engaged life in the world, not a life under the Rule, nor a regular life, but life in the world.

His public life was naturally quite different. The three years

that followed, the three last years. It was quite different because it was a public life, a life of preaching. But in that life
which is not so to say imitable, except in a subsidiary sense,
a secondary sense, what is the direction of the movement?
Is it a retreat, a withdrawal upon oneself, a retreat, a movement in the opposite direction toward the Rule, away from
the world, toward what ought to be the Rule? On the contrary, as you know, it was a powerful, an infinite movement
toward the world. Toward what was already, what has always
been the world, the age, me, for I am age itself and antiquity.

Such was the foundation, the Christian institution, the *mystique;* the original, first state, the pure state of mysticism, such
was in a sense its future; such was its technique, the mechanism of the *mystique.* An immense, a perpetual, inexhaustible,
imperishable source, a mystical source nourished by itself,
feeding itself, emerging, springing up, bursting out during
those three years, those three temporal years, and flowing into
the world.

Those, my friends, were the first years of the Church, temporal, worldly, historical years, historical but also mystical.
My friend, I look in vain for the Rule, for what was subsequently the Rule; you will not find the origin or any trace of
the Rule there. I don't see the shadow of a rule, the trace of a
beginning of the Rule. I can't discover the foundation of the
Rule, of any Rule.

A mystical spring flowed, a source of love, of life, of grace,
during those years: an eternal spring, toward the sands of the
age; an inexhaustible, vivifying spring, nourishing the world,
overflowing on to the age, penetrating, inundating the world;
a mystical spring temporally in the world, flowing and over-

flowing toward it. Who can tell you, who will give you back the three years of *that* history, those historic years, the years of Jesus's preachings? You know how inadequate I am. I am only a poor woman. A very poor woman in fact. All I can do, as you know, is to register a few results. When they are over, fixed, pigeon-holed, filed, catalogued — when they are quite dead. You have said it often enough, you rascal, my dear child; you have let it out often enough, you wretch: fragmentary, fragments, ashes, the trace of puffs of smoke. I know it by heart, because I, history, know so much by heart. You have repeated it often enough, and with such anger, that there must be a little truth in it.

I look in vain for the Rule. What I see is a *foundation* in the world, in the matter of the age, in and toward the world; the foundation of a city in the world itself, of which the world is the matter and the price; the foundation of a mystical city working for the world, for eternity, working the material, forming it for eternity; in fact, the foundation of the City of God, of the eternal city, God's eternal city. Not the foundation of the Rule, but a very different foundation. And consequently, my friend, an entirely different *mystique*, infinitely different; an entirely different mystical technique; a perfect mechanism, I need hardly tell you, faultless, impeccable I need hardly add, since it was the technique of Jesus himself; his technique and mechanism.

There was no separation between the world and the Rule. Only an intimate and continual penetration, a compenetration, an infusion always moving in the same direction, a continuous arterial irrigation of arterial blood by spiritual blood, penetrating the tissues themselves. Always moving in the same direction, a source of movement and life and grace.

But the fact is that I, history, cannot grasp movements. No, I simply cannot. You see, I am not a bergsonian. Though there are plenty of ladies without me, who are bergsonians. I don't want to be just another bergsonian woman. And then it would irritate Benda.[3] Movements are not my business. Not my style. They do not match my style of beauty. And, in any case, it is not my *métier*. You have said it only too often: I am a woman who notes things down. All I need is a *guichet*, a little *guichet* and some pigeon-holes. I am the chief clerk of all those employed in cataloguing, filing and registration. Reality and movement are not my business.

I do not drink at the source, the fountain head. I only drink filtered water, and one cannot have too many filters. The flood of movement, the moving flood of reality, the movement of life and of living reality is not in my department. It only confuses me. It looks so flexible, so elastic to me; it runs like syrup; it is positively syrupy; and produces such undulating rhythms that it makes me giddy, turns my stomach. But what do you expect, I am history, and everyone knows me for what I am. They must take me as I am. I am ready-made, prefabricated. You must accept me in advance.

Three luminous years illuminated my night. Never, my friend, shall I give you the history of those three years. I shall never portray their history *historically* for you. Those who have tried to do so, purely historically, according to me,

3. Julien Benda, author of *La Trahison des Clercs.*

have never, alas, produced anything but some rather indifferent daubs. Thus we sail between two curés; we maneuver between two groups of curés: the lay curés and the ecclesiastical
curés; the clerical and the anticlerical curés; the lay curés who
deny the eternal aspect of the temporal, who would like to extract the eternal from the temporal, remove the eternal from
the temporal; and the ecclesiastical curés who deny the temporal in the eternal, who would like to remove the temporal
from the eternal.

Neither of them are Christian, since the Christian technique, the mechanism of its technique consists in the engagement of the one in the other, in their being dovetailed one into
the other, in gear, united, unique and reciprocal. The temporal
in the eternal and (what is more usually denied, and which is
in fact the truly marvellous thing) the eternal in the temporal.
So that neither are Christian.

To discover which of the two is the less Christian is a nice
point. It is always difficult and almost always impossible, alas,
to know which is the less Christian. I suspect that it is really
a problem beyond the scope of history; but speaking beyond
my competence, I lean, unfortunately, to the opinion that it
is the ecclesiastical curés who are, in fact, the less Christian.

Those who try to extract the eternal from the temporal inevitably fall into some sort of materialism (since it has been
agreed to fall into it), into a crude, into the lowest form of
materialism. That is not the real great danger. What I mean
is that it is not an extraordinary form of danger, an infinite
danger. Materialism has its *mystique*. Of all philosophical systems it is perhaps the one which has most, certainly the one
which needs most *mystique*, which wants it most, which *lacks*

it most. In a sense. But it is a *mystique* of a particular kind, and it is not (very) dangerous. It does not touch, it has not the prestige to affect, the tender or anxious soul (the gentle soul), the deep soul, and it holds no attraction for the properly mystical soul, the soul predestined to Christianity, the ante-Christian souls of those who are Christian in advance. It is inoffensive, large, heavy, ponderous, crude. It is not relatively (very) dangerous.

The opposite *mystique*, on the contrary, is altogether different. The *mystique* that denies the temporal in the eternal, that dissociates the temporal from the eternal is strictly speaking anti-Christian: falls into or rises up to — whichever you like — attains, a *mystique* which is anti-Christian. For that particular kind of involvement, that insertion of the temporal in the eternal and of the eternal in the temporal, that incredible interlocking is the very heart and *foundation* of Christianity, of its mechanism, its technique and its institution.

Otherwise one falls into *mystiques* which are particularly dangerous, because they tempt and seduce noble minds, souls one would have thought (pre)destined for the Christian vocation. Otherwise one aspires to those vague spiritualities: idealisms, immaterialisms, religiosities, pantheisms, philosophisms which are dangerous because they are not clumsy and not crude, and falls into vague mysticism. And there you meet competition. You can be harmed and lost. That, unfortunately, is generally the situation of the clerks. I mean of the good ones. For the rest, the great majority today, almost the whole lot at present, though perhaps rather less since the Separation of Church and State, a little more than just after the Separation, are up to their necks in the world.

To deny the eternal, my friend, to *found* the world on matter, on simple matter, on naked, unknown, (scientifically) unknowable matter, to found the whole world on the temporal, the great world on me, little history, the power of the whole creation on me, *la belle qui fut heaulmière,* is such a hazardous undertaking, my child, that it is harmless; it is safeguarded by its singularity, by its crudeness. It is an improbable *hypothesis*, as they say, a strange fantasy. Hardly even a thesis, it is so crude. A very curious idea, you will surely agree, which would occur to no one who had seen me. It is not genuine competition. It works in a field which is not ours, which is not interesting. It only catches those who want to be caught, who are already caught, beforehand. Not very dangerous; not very interesting, nor moving either.

But the other hypothesis, the opposite, antagonistic, hypothesis! How fine, how noble, how great, how aristocratic even, socially speaking! How beautiful! What a magnificent, subtle and cultivated hypothesis! It therefore offers very dangerous competition. It works in the field we are interested in, our field. On the souls we work upon, and often tears them away from us. It is false and seductive.

To deny me, my friend, to treat me with contempt — what a temptation, what a (fatal) slope to be on. And so we are still steering between the two curés: those who deny the eternal; and those who deny me temporality; those who make me everything; and those who make me nothing. Nothing at all. When I am so little.

Which of the two, at the present time, is the worse, the more unbearable, we can now discuss, and now that we are entering the field of history, we can have a good talk. My competence in this matter is not in doubt. You ask me which is the more detestable. But both, my child, both are the more detestable.

Come now, *Madame*, come now, you who have known so many of them!

My child, they are all the most loathsome.

Still, *Madame*, still, one must choose, after all, one must choose.

Well, dear child — well, then, one must choose. Well, if one has to choose, then it depends when, under whom.

Under Combes, my child, it is the lay curé who is the more loathsome. He makes himself so unbearable, so unendurable that you cannot imagine how the ecclesiastical curés could be as odious, how they could become as odious, how they could manage such a *tour de force*. How they could do the trick. But don't worry, my child, don't worry, my poor weak child. Leave things alone, let time run on, and you will see that, under MacMahon, the ecclesiastical curé is the more detestable. The more unbearable, the more unpleasant, the more odious. And that they succeed in being so with an unction quite beyond the powers of the others. With that hard unction, that unctuous hardness, their particular unction and hardness. Just wait and see. Wait and see. You will see those days again. And they will be the same as ever.

Once again, in the midst of the insecurity of the modern world, in the midst of its vanity and inadequacy and the scandalous emptiness of its doctrines, surrounded by sterility, futility, irreality, the old trunk will once again put forth buds and leaves and branches, the old trunk will flower and bear fruit. Grace will once again be at work. Once again, my friend, it is already working. It has worked. And once again, my friend, the curés will think it is all for their benefit. They will think, once again; they are already thinking; it's already done. They used to believe; they have begun to believe again. That God is their beater, theirs alone. His sole occupation is beating for them, recruiting for them, like a press gang. He does nothing else. He is their recruiting sergeant. And they are pretty tough with him.

You ask me which is the more hateful. But not for long. You will find them again. You have already found them. The good thing, the nice thing about the curés is that when one comes across them again after thirty years they are still the same, just the same, just as odious as before. Where the lay curés are concerned there is this to be said: at least they do not invoke the religion they are destroying. Which they have undertaken to destroy. They despise it openly and that is partly what wounds us. But it is the others who wound us deeply. They invoke the religion they are demolishing so efficiently. They feed on it — one of the most beautiful, the most perfect historical examples of political, social, physiological and sociological parasitism in existence.

But that greater hatefulness — believe me, my friend, I often have to do it — only translates a greater religious hatefulness, historically, into the temporal event, bearing on the object of faith; and, not to mince words, indicates the greater heresy. For everything depends upon that mortice, that dovetailing of the temporal and the eternal. Everything collapses once that adjustment is unsettled, or out of the true, or taken to pieces. The very center: that is what it is, the engagement of the eternal in the temporal. Do away with that link and there is nothing left. No world to save. No souls to save. No Christianity left. It is divorced from its technique. There is neither temptation nor salvation, neither trial nor time nor anything. There is no incarnation, nor redemption nor creation itself. Neither Jews nor Christians. Neither promises nor promises fulfilled. Nothing but smoke and shadow.

That, my friend, is what comes of despising me. You begin to see how important I am. Otherwise it would have been so simple. God had only to remain in his heaven, before the creation; so peaceful. He did not need us. And Jesus had only to remain (quite) quietly in heaven, before that central, that axial, vital part of the creation, before the incarnation, the redemption. Why did he come, why did the world come? One can only suppose that I have a certain importance, my friend, me, a woman of no importance. And then there would not have been the fall, of the angels, of man, neither fall nor redemption. There would be no history, nothing to bother about. Everyone remaining quietly at home. Just think of my importance, if it is I who have got so many people on the move, disturbed so many people, so many important people. To have started so tragic a story. God, my friend, a God sacrificed himself on my account. There is (some) Christianity for you. There you have its point of origin, the whole mechanism assembled. The rest is what Thucydides called *de la fichaise;* in Greek, less than nothing.

The least of sinners, the least of sins, wounds Jesus eternally. There you have Christianity. And I, history, throughout my long history, can do nothing which does not interest Jesus, God, naturally and as though physically. I cannot commit anything temporally which is not inserted, physically as it were, into the body of God himself. There, my child, is Christianity for you. Real. The rest, my friend, all the rest — come, my dear Alphandry, come now, let us say the rest is good enough for the comparative history of religions. It is the binding, the eternal, temporal binding, the link, the inlay of the one in the other, that incrucification as it were, which makes Christianity. The rest is good material for schoolmasters.

Otherwise it would not have been worthwhile, taking so much trouble.

The Christian, my friend, is profoundly human; he is even, absolutely, all that is most human. For he alone reckons humanity at the price of God. Man, the least of sinners, the most miserable of sinners, at the price of God. He has entered the very heart of humanity. He is literally at the heart and core of the tree. For one must be careful to observe, and this is what we have to show in many forms, what we have been saying — the sinner is literally and strictly speaking no less Christian than the saint. He is no less indispensable to the functioning of the mechanism. Jesus came and suffered for the sinner no less than for the saint (nor must one fall into the opposite exaggeration and heresy which by an abuse of humility consists in saying that Jesus came and suffered more for the sinner than for the saint). Don't let's exaggerate. He came equally for both equally. Let us say that he came (equally) for everyone and that we are at the axis of Christianity. He came to save the (whole) world, my child.

Here, my child, in a new form, in a personal form, in the form of the workers of every hour, of the first and the eleventh hour, in the aspect of *citizens*, we find the same general situation we have found in so many other cases. It is, no doubt, a great temptation to be more Christian than the Christians,

and to reinforce it with humility, so to speak; to exaggerate
and exasperate that virtue (in the belief that one is strengthening it) and to enjoy it and abuse it, to carry it to excess in
the case of trials and suffering. It is one way of falling off, on
the right side. But falling nevertheless. Being too Christian.
Going down to the floor below, or up to the floor above. The
temptation is indeed great. Forgive me, my child, excuse me,
but one must distinguish. One can (not) be too saintly. Because there is a model one can never attain, Jesus Christ. The
imitation of Jesus Christ. But one can be too Christian. And
not Christian enough. That is to say, one can go too far up
or too far down, in a certain house; and in a certain mechanism, where everything depends upon equilibrium, a unique,
given, revealing equilibrium, one can increase the importance
of a particular part, exaggerate the importance of one or two
pieces and falsify both. That, my friend, is not Christianity.
Christianity is a certain level, a certain floor, not a half-way
house, but an axial floor, central, fixed, where one has to fix
oneself. But in one sense the sinner does not inhabit the floor
any less than the saint; he functions no less in the whole system; he is no less essential. There you have the axis. Equally,
or rather together. Communally. In common. In community.
In communion.

Those who tend to exaggerate humility and reinforce
Christianity, and perfect it, and make themselves more Christian, let them beware, my friend, let them take care. The evil
one is cunning. The temptation is great. It is the temptation
of good Christians. But it will not have escaped you, and you
will easily see what we historians take in at a glance, what we
unearth at once, for we are formed by habit, by our studies

and essays and *Beiträge;* and what is obvious to us owing to our professional skill, our powers of diagnosis, our ability in following the vein in the marble even under the most diffi-cult conditions. You, too, will see a single, the same inclina-tion (this is where one must begin), the same thought, idea, and sometimes, when it becomes more ingrained, the same sentiment, the same virtue, the same sin, the same grace. The same acts and the same operations. It will not have escaped you that these perfectionists might well belong to the cult of progress, where religion is concerned, which is the great mod-ern heresy and irreligion. To the one and only cult of progress. They would like to make Christianity progress. But beware. They make it so in a way that will cost them dear. Christianity is not a progressive religion of progress. And therefore in no sense an historical religion. It is, one is ashamed to have to repeat such primary truths, it is a mystical religion.

How curious, is it not: a mystical religion; instead of being an intellectual religion, a religion for intellectuals. That is what upsets your history of comparative religions. It is a mys-tical religion. The religion of salvation. Those great perfec-tionists, those amateurs, in a word, those partisans, those par-tisans of progress who want to improve Christianity, may well be men of (too) good will, zealots, champions of the religion of progress. In the last analysis. So that they are really decen-tralized Christians — Christians off center. They have come adrift from Christianity. They would do better to adhere to it again. That is to say, they are no longer Christians, and per-haps simply moderns, strictly speaking moderns, if, as we have said, Christianity is essentially an equilibrium, firm, fixed at the center, at the very axis of those two parts. There is no question of perfecting it. It is a matter of holding, of sticking to the fixed point. And when one has tried, one sees it isn't quite so easy. Look, my friend, let us stick to the fixed point.

There are people who want to perfect Christianity. It is rather like wanting to perfect the North. How clever they are. Directions, my child, are given: the North, for example, in the physical world, and Christianity in the mystical world. The North in astronomy, Christianity in mysticism. The North is pretty well fixed in physics in general; Christianity is fixed, mystically fixed. The North is naturally fixed; Christianity is naturally, and supernaturally, fixed. Thus, certain points being given and fixed, the whole thing is to observe them. Instead of improving upon them.

The fixed point of Christianity is that there is a certain floor level, a house *ni si haut ni si bas enfant de la terre* where dwell both sinner and saint. Both equally, in a certain sense, forming part, an integral, an integrating part of the same system, or better still of the same city; cocitizens of the same City of God, my friend, of the same eternal city; the same eternal city temporally *founded*.

Sin, my child, is not foreign to Christianity, far from it. It is of course contrary to sanctity, which is quite another matter, quite a different thing, a different operation, and action. A completely different outlook and situation. But strictly speaking it is literally true to say that it is Christianity which posits sin (the Christian system, the mechanism and technique of Christianity, the mystique of Christianity), and that without Christianity there would be no sins, because there would be no sin. There would be everything else, every sort and kind of thing, the whole gamut of human crimes and faults, vices and errors, a host, an army, a flood impossible to estimate. And on the other side too there would, without doubt, be an innumerable army of virtues and goodness, truths and heroism, heroic virtues, human kindness and pity, impossible to compute. But on the one side sanctity would be lacking; on the other side sin would be lacking. For they are both equally Christian, professionally, technically, so to say, Christian. On the good side, if I may so express it, there would be all the goodness and beauty and truth and the rest, everything you like, everything you can imagine, everything human and humane, all the humanities; but there would simply not be sanctity. And on the bad side there would be all the crimes; but sin would be lacking. Sanctity and its complement, its contrary, its limitation, sin, its contrary complement, are essential parts of the Christian system, the proper invention of Christianity. Without Christianity there would have been everything else.

When therefore we speak of de-Christianization, when we take note of the disaster, we must agree about terms, we must have the courage to define and agree. Sinner and saint are both proper to Christianity, two effects, two results, two final and efficient causes, two creations. When we say that the world is being de-Christianized, when we watch and take note of the disaster, when we note the fact that the modern world is all that is most contrary to what is Christian, in its very root, we must be careful what we say; we must not draw back before what we are going to say. We do not in the least mean that within the Christian system sanctity is once again submerged beneath sin — that would be almost insignificant by comparison, even though it were much more serious this time, in quality, in gravity, infinitely more serious than ever before.

That, you understand, my child — now listen carefully to what I am saying — that would be nothing. What we are saying, what we are commenting upon is infinitely more serious. In a sense the only serious thing. But we must not draw back.

What we mean is not that one of the (two) parts of the system has invaded the other, more or less, reinvaded it, altogether invaded it. That would be nothing. We are accustomed to that, and it was always the same part which invaded, again and again. What we mean is that the modern world obviously renounces the whole system, both parts together and their interplay. That is what we mean when we say that the world is being de-Christianized, and we affirm the disaster.

That is what so many Christians, and notably so many Catholics, well intentioned at that, will not admit and do not want to see. And that falsehood, that cowardly perversion, that sin, prevent them from usefully employing themselves in retarding it, from saving anything. That incurably cowardly diagnosis results in an incurably cowardly cure. In a cowardly prayer, a cowardly charity, a cowardly faith, a cowardly success, a cowardly respect, a cowardly government, a cowardly *mystique*. It is true they do not want to avow, and will never admit that the de-Christianization, indeed the whole disaster, comes from the clerks. A fundamental fault in the *mystique* involves a fundamentally cowardly *mystique*.

What we mean is that the modern world has given up, renounced the whole system, the whole *mystique*. Which means that from now on there is a new and different world; that the modern world is not just a bad Christian world, which would be nothing, but an unchristian world, literally, absolutely, totally de-Christianized. That is what it means. That is what needs to be said and seen. If it were only the old story, if it was merely that sin had once again encroached, it would mean nothing, my dear child; we are used to that, the world is used to it. One more bad Christian century after many others. If people knew history as well as I do, they would know perhaps that it has always been so, that all those twenty centuries have really been centuries of miserable Christianity, evil centuries, terribly wanting in mysticism. Which means that the contingent of saints has always been minute compared with the sinners. And while, no doubt, a few saints triumphed eternally, no doubt, whole masses, whole peoples of sinners held power and dominated temporally; while a few saints saved themselves eternally (and others too perhaps), and made their salvation eternal, the sinners, the innumerable sinners risked temporally being lost. That, alas, is unfortunately the *régime* itself. Those were Christian miseries. And the grandeur of Christianity too. But the *régime* is no more, and the disaster is that even our miseries are no longer Christian. That is the truth of it. That is what is new. As long as our misery was a Christian misery, as long as vices created sins, and what was base was also Christian, as long as crime meant perdition, there was, so to speak, something good about it. You see what I mean, my friend. There was some hope, there was something; there was matter for grace, naturally. Whereas nowadays everything is new and everything is different. Everything is modern. That is what one must see. What must be said. Everything is completely unchristian. Alas, alas, if it were merely bad Christianity, one could see a way out, one could begin to talk. But when we talk of de-Christianization, when one says there is a modern world, and that it is completely de-Christianized, that simply means that it has given up the whole system altogether, that it moves and has its being outside the system; it means that everybody has renounced the whole of Christianity. It implies the constitution of a totally different, new, free, entirely independent system. Were it only bad Christianity, my child, it would not (yet) be very interesting; it would no longer be interesting. You understand, my poor, dear friend, what I am driving at.

What is interesting, what is new, is that there is no longer any Christianity left. That expresses not only the extent but the nature of the disaster. Once the Catholics have consented to see and measure and admit the disaster and where it comes from, once they have given up their cowardly diagnosis, then, and only then will they perhaps be able to work usefully; then they will no longer be lazy, and we shall, perhaps, be able to talk. But what they will not recognize, what is new and interesting, alas, my son, alas, you know what I mean, is that there is a modern world, a modern society (I do not say a modern city, and as the song says: "You know what I mean"), is that that world, that society, has constituted itself entirely exteriorly outside Christianity. For it is no longer a question of internal difficulties, but of something complete and exterior; not even of an exterior difficulty, which would still imply some relationship, some link, but on the contrary, of a complete absence of relationship, of link, of binding, and even in point of fact of difficulties; a very curious lack therefore, very disturbing, in the highest degree unsettling: a mutual, reciprocal independence, very singular and strange.

My child, we have seen a world, a society, I do not say a city, a perfectly viable and entirely unchristian society instituted, if not *founded*, under our very eyes; seen it being established, functioning, living. That must be conceded. Those who deny it are hopeless. And just as the world, as I, history, had seen the world, whole worlds, whole humanities live and prosper before Jesus, so we have the sorrow of seeing whole worlds, humanities, living and prospering *after* Jesus. Both the ones and the others without Jesus. Just as one has seen whole worlds, whole *cities* founded, born, assembled, prosper and increase and decrease, like plants, be born and die unchristian, *ante*-Christian, so we, the first, have seen, the first since Jesus, and see every day, a whole world, if not a city, a wholly unchristian, post-Christian society, be born and grow and not decrease, prosper and not perish. And between the two there is a chasm.

That the world should have lived without Jesus, before Jesus, seems to us perfectly natural, and in effect it is in the natural order. It fits quite easily into our notions of time, order, history, development, of events in time. It fits well enough into our idea of the *before* coming before the *after* and the *after* after the *before*. It does not surprise us too much. And then we have learned it all in history, when we were small, so it seems natural to us. It forms an integral part of a common domain, of common memory and of the history of the human community. Everything that belongs to the past, all that we have learned in history (and which is therefore twice past, as it were, once in history, once in the teaching of history), in history books, when we were young, seems to have been acquired naturally, as it should be. But in reality one of the most difficult problems, full of mystery and a source of distress, is that Jesus should have come so late in the history of man and humanity; that the incarnate should have come so late, and that the incarnation and redemption, those two essential operators, the one bringing forth the other, the one announcing the other, should have come so late; that such a lapse of time should have passed between the fall and the redemption; that so many centuries should have intervened; that so many peoples and civilizations, some of them in a certain sense successful, prosperous cultures, societies, empires (in itself nothing), but cities, which is saying a lot, if not everything, and some of them successful in almost every way, that so many antecedent humanities, such considerable and important parts of humanity should have been able to live, unchristian and ante-Christian, before Jesus and without Jesus; that so many should have been born after the fall and before the redemption, in error and without redemption; that Jesus should have come so long after Adam; that so many souls, so many civic souls and citizens, some of them successful in so many ways, if not in most ways, some of the finest, the highest, wisest, most heroic the earth has ever borne, that ever flowered in the gardens of the cities of the earth; that so many memorable souls (temporally immortal) should have come into the world and died *before;* that Jesus should have come so long after Adam. . . . That, my friend, is one of the disturbing questions.

That, my friend, is one of the most disquieting problems. That so many souls should have been situated just there, in that yawning chasm of history. That they should have been posted to that strange post, forced to be born, live and die in that interval, commissioned to hold the boards, to *occupy* the stage of history between the prologue and the first act, during that unprofitable interval. And sometimes (for there have been some great buffoons) to amuse the groundlings. And that there should have been such an interval. And that there should have been so many involved. But there, no one thinks about it. They prefer not to. It's a habit. A habit not to think about it. About anything. It's soon done. It's laziness, common laziness, the great cowardice.

To think. In reality, if you like, if one thought about it, it is one of those apparent, very apparent injustices, a problem which confounds one. To think that it could have been done, that it could have happened; that there should have been such a time, an intercostal time!

We console ourselves vaguely (after the event, and all the more easily since we are not involved); the old egoism plays its part, has only to play its part; it is waiting at the door and needs no efficient cause; it is sufficient for the obstacle to fall, for the door to open. Our old egoism is at the door, as it always is, waiting for its cue; we console ourselves generously, liberally, all the more so when we think we are no longer directly concerned; so we console ourselves vaguely with the idea that it was in the days of the Old Law. (And as we belong to the New Law things are clearly quite different.) And finally we console ourselves very sincerely because, in the same way that those times and peoples, those souls and facts, had to *furnish* history, habitable history and the centuries and space and spacing of the centuries, so in the same way, from where we stand in history today, we see that time itself was furnished, as it were, by the prophets. The prophets, one after another, that beautiful long avenue leading up to the mansion, that lovely avenue of poplars, perfectly aligned. Some, my dear Lévy, are taller than others: the tops are uneven, the trunks are not all of the same strength, and not all are lost in the clouds, not all reach the sky. But the foot of each tree is planted in such a way that they all, equally, announce the master's mansion, the castle. As for us, we see and know the prophets. But we know them after the event, from the other end, after the termination, after the achievement, the arrival, from the other side of the arrival.

We know that long, long-suffering line of prophets, that triumphant line of prophets, the procession which walks ahead, and those who walk after them, and the one who walks immediately ahead of them, the forerunner in fact; we take in the procession at a glance, we know their greatness and their height and their travels. But we see it from the other end, with a backward look. With an eye, which in a sense comes from the other world.

And today, we who are in our father's house, who have arrived, for whom someone has arrived, and who on arriving tasted the fresh water and the fresh bread, who have drunk at the source from the hollow of our hands, who live unworthy in the rooms of the mansion, we who have our beds in the rooms and our place assigned to us at the common table, we walk in the gardens of the house, in those wonderful gardens, admiring the paths, the neat beds, the flower garden and the vegetable garden and the orchard with its fruit, and the park too, the beautiful shady park, surrounded by old walls and a dyke (one can climb over) and the farm buildings near the mansion and the arable fields, ploughed, ready for the wheat and the beans; and living in the house we vaguely recall that there is an avenue.

On the other side of the house and the farm, perceived dimly, perhaps no more than a memory, on the other side of

the village, preceding, announcing the façade (yes, that is it),
we perceive, we know there is an avenue. And then, full of
courage, retrospective courage, full of confidence, retrospective confidence, we who are unworthy, suddenly feel full of
courage and confidence and patience for the men of the avenue, for those poplars. Looking back, our courage is unshak-
able and nothing disturbs our confidence. Our patience is inexhaustible. But we forget, we like to forget that we are the
unworthy inhabitants of the house, that we saw it being built,
by our fathers for us and before us, that we know when and
how it was built, and that the avenue, on the contrary, had
already lasted a thousand years. By such means, good, bad,
indifferent, we end by reassuring ourselves more or less, in our
egoism, and by convincing ourselves that it is perfectly natural. But in reality it is not merely a disconcerting problem, a
terrifying one; it utterly confounds one: the fact of those three
thousand years, and one must count carefully, those five thousand years of society, of cities, of humanity; that they should
have been thrown into the pit, that there should have been so
many anterior souls, ante-Christian souls: before Jesus, without Jesus. But I admit, and it must be admitted, the problem
which confounds one is child's play compared to the problem
which confronts our generation. And to be more precise, the
generation which has watched the inauguration of the modern
world, the establishment of the government of the intellectual party in the modern world. For the first time since Jesus,
we have seen, under our very eyes, we have just seen a new
world arise, if not a city; a new society formed, if not a city;
modern society, the modern world; a world, a society, constituted, or at any rate assembled (born) and grow, after Jesus

and without Jesus. And what is more, my friend, and it cannot be denied, it has succeeded.

That, my child, is what gives your generation, and the times in which we live, a capital importance; that is what places you at a unique point in the world's history, in the events of the history of the world. That is what puts you in a uniquely tragic position. You are the first. You are the first moderns. You are the first under whom, before whom, under whose eyes has been set up, and who yourselves have set up, the government of the intellectual party in the modern world. And what gives that fact and gives you such a capital importance, you, your world, your party, what gives infinite weight and gravity to our times, adds poignancy and seriousness to the problem, is that you are on the threshold of a new event, that you are the first inaugurators, under whom and before whom and by whom a new thing has been done, for you are the first to have succeeded in making a world, and a prosperous world, without Jesus; a whole society, a prosperous society, without Jesus; a world, a society that is prosperous and unchristian after Jesus.

That, my poor child, is what you must see. That is what must be admitted. That is all you have to read on the lips of events. That is what the priests will never see; what they refuse to see; what they will not say; what the clerks obstinately deny; and what so many Catholics follow them in disavowing; what following in their footsteps all Catholics deny. Obstinately, no less obstinately, than the clerks.

What would they not do to mask and evade the truth, the reality, what would the Catholics not do, with the clerks in their midst, in order not to say their *mea culpa*, they who have made so many others say it?

They begin by denying the fact that stares them in the face, by remaining silent, and blinding themselves (figuratively of course or it would hurt), by lying and denying the evidence, the disaster. And then by a singular contradiction, which proves at bottom how guilty they feel, they formally and officially, superficially and pompously, announce that all is well, that all is as it should be, and at the same time complain without ceasing. They complain, whine and curse, and are thoroughly unbearable, and incriminate the age, the world, from habit, citing the evils of the times. Not with much conviction either, but like a scout complaining of the bad weather.

There was bad weather too, a storm even, on the lake of Tiberias and Peter was already complaining that he would never be able to catch any fish. He even alleged they would perish.

Under the Romans too, times were bad. But Jesus did not hide away. He did not declare himself ready to give up. He did not take refuge behind the wickedness of the times.

There are even some very striking analogies between Roman days and ours, between Roman times and the times that have become modern. More than a mere resemblance, more than a curious analogy; a sort of similarity of movement. One might say that everything was ready in the Roman world, ready for the start, prepared in the fullness of the Roman domination, in the Roman peace, in that Mediterranean world pacified by the Empire, in Gaul and Spain and the Germanies and the Britannies, in the appeasement of the Greek world, and in the semioriental, semioccidental world; in the decadence of Greek thought, in the lack of intelligence, the mis-intelligence, the misunderstanding and lack of understanding in Greek thought; or rather in that triple decadence of Greek thought becoming anaemic at the center, wasting away, growing thinner, subtler, overrefined, exasperating itself, ossified in its refinements and in the subtleties of Alexandrian philosophy and civilization; softened by the softness of oriental corruption and at the same time hardened through its contact with Roman hardness, hardening under the military yoke, under the imperial rule, the servitude, under masters whose strength did not lie entirely in the intelligence, at the contact with harsh customs and rough masters. (There has never been such a good example of the fact that there is no such thing as an arithmetic mean of qualities, and of the fact that such language must be reserved for quantities. The softness on the one side, and the hardness on the other, never mixed, or combined as they say in chemistry, to form firmness.) But in that triple decadence it seems as though everything were prepared for the modern world to make its start; there was the same disorder and the same type of disintelligence. Everything was prepared. But Jesus came. He had three years to do. He did his three years. But he did not waste time complaining and invoking the evils of the times. The modern world was about to come and was prepared. He cut it short. Very simply. By making Christianity. By interpolating the Christian world.

He did not accuse or incriminate anyone. He saved.

He did not incriminate the world. He saved the world.

They (the others) vituperate and incriminate. Vituperative doctors who blame the patient. They accuse the sands of the world, but in Jesus's day too, there was the world and the sands of the world. But in those arid sands, out of that arid century, sprang the unquenchable spring of grace.

Oh, no, they do not *imitate* Jesus.

They feel, they know from the texts, that the world has been confided to their care, and seeing the condition it is in, and the state to which they have reduced it, seeing what they have done to the world committed to their care, those doctors turn on their patient: vituperative pastors who take it out on the flock. They will do anything to deny the disaster.

The disaster is in fact a double one. There is first of all the cosmic disaster as it were, the geographic disaster, in the sense that whole parts of the globe have ignored the world of Jesus, and one cannot really see today how they could be tackled when we are retreating on our own ground, from which we have been driven out, so to speak. Jesus, without a doubt, came to save the world. The first disaster is that Christianity did not "take" on the whole habitable earth, the catholic, ecumenical earth; far from it indeed: it did not take except in certain parts and those not the most considerable in extent, in volume, in weight, in numbers and surface. The first disaster is that there were so many peoples, so many souls where Christianity got no reaction; so many *who did not feel any the worse for it,* and there, my friend, there unfortunately is the secret, the heart of the mystery.

My friend, one must classify mystery itself. Jesus came to save the world. There can be no doubt of that. And given that fact there are three mysteries, or to speak more exactly, three mysteries of exceptional difficulty.

Let us begin by classifying what is not a mystery, to clear the way, and get it out of the argument; because it is anterior to the point at issue; an anterior, and above all, an interior question. Jesus having come to save the world, it remains a mystery why souls are lost, or at least have that appearance. But that infinite anguish, to which the saints were never resigned, to which we can never know that Jesus was resigned, is nevertheless a classified anguish, if you will allow me to say so; and you can see what I mean. We know where it is. We know where to receive it. As long as it is a matter of individual souls losing themselves, within a Christian people, it remains an interior problem; an interior anguish, an internal matter. It is known and classified, alas. Even catalogued. It does not overflow Christianity. It is internal. I mean, alas, that we know how to take it, we know its infinite price. We know what we have to deal with. Twenty centuries of Christianity have created, formed, instituted a sort of rite or ritual for that anguish. They have accustomed us to it and have provided a mechanism, so to speak, for dealing with it. It is properly speaking a Christian problem, eminently Christian. A problem which is of infinite price and yet quite ordinary, for that is normal in Christianity, which *has set an infinite price on everything,* has put up the price everywhere in the market of values. Thus it is not a problem which suggests the idea of a fault in technique (the Christian technique), or that a fault has been committed at the very heart of Christianity. It is a preliminary problem coming before the threshold of our problem. It would require twenty volumes, my friend. And above all, prayer. We shall not eliminate it, but "preliminate" it. On the contrary, it is we, in a way, who will be eliminated from it. But immediately after comes the threshold.

Immediately after the threshold, is quite a different problem, my child, and I would add that it is a historical problem. The problem we were discussing was in fact an administrative problem. Not that I claim to reduce its importance. But it is in fact an internal problem. Alas, it is a question of knowing why and how there were bad citizens in the city; in the Christian city, which had been *founded*. A poignant problem, but one which no longer disconcerts us, no longer throws us off our balance. It ought to disconcert us, but it does not. In fact. Because we are accustomed. Because we are thick-skinned. And moreover, to speak accurately, the wicked citizens are never put outside the city. There is literally no exile from that city. One is never put outside it. Excommunication puts the faithful out of communion. In a certain sense, if one likes, puts them outside the Church. But one must be careful, and pay attention. It does not put them outside Christianity. It puts them outside Christendom, so to speak, but not outside Christianity, far from it, in the sense that it does not put them out of play, in balk, outside the system and its functioning. Since it does not put them beyond the penalties which are an integral part of the system. It is, on the contrary, one of the points of the system that works best, most fully, strikes hardest and perhaps most brutally, most directly, normally, straight. Nothing is so characteristic of a system, nothing reveals and discloses a system, alas, so much as the penalties which it entails. The excommunicate is not ex-Christianized, not unchristian or ante-Christian or post-Christian. He is not an ancient or a modern. And reciprocally the ancient and the modern, the ante-Christian and the post-Christian is not excommunicate, but he is not Christian. And, in fact, he is not excommunicate because he is not Christian.

It is a different order, a different register.

The problem of de-Christianization is a totally different

one. That is what Christians, notably the Catholics, will not see. And as long as they will not see it or admit it, they work and pray in vain; their work is in vain, the little work they do; and their prayers are in vain, the few prayers they say.

For alas, when they work and pray, they attack the new problem as if it were the old problem, confusing the new problem with the old problem. They imagine it is the same, that the situation is the same, and they say, to themselves and one another, that modern man is a sinful Christian, in a state of sin; that the whole modern thing is vaguely, confusedly, diffusely sinful, like a stain that has soaked into the wood; and that while the world until now was painted with sin, in the color of sin, today, on the contrary, it is *stained,* and the stain has sunk in everywhere, almost as though it were a sort of latent state, everywhere, soaking into the fiber of the wood. The modern world would, according to them, be a (Christian) world stained with sin.

To hold to that point of view is to commit the grossest of errors deliberately. When it is a completely different problem. The real problem is that the modern world is an unchristian world, *which has succeeded perfectly well in doing without Christianity.*

The Christian cannot become unchristian; the sinner, even the excommunicate, the reprobate, cannot become non-Christian. That is a totally different state. Christianity is indelible. That is precisely what is said, in another form, in Christian technical language, in canonical form, in theological language; when one says that the sacraments are indelible. That is the language of the priest and of the Church.

One must distinguish. There are several kinds of sacrament,

several families (classes almost), different groups: first of all,
at the head, the essential sacrament, essential, nourishing, the
sacrament of life, mystically nourishing, the carnal, spiritual,
temporal and eternal nourishment; the sacrament of communion, strictly speaking nourishing, nutritive, alimentary. Secondly, subsidiarily, the sacrament of purgation, of ablution:
primitively, perhaps, a disciplinary sacrament, a sort of communion, but no longer carnal, interior, or mystical, but social,
interiorly exterior, exterior to the soul, interior for the Church,
in the Church; but nowadays it is almost exclusively regarded
as anterior, preparatory, not so much to communion as to each
communion; thus a great honor has been done to it, an ag-
grandizement. But all the other sacraments are indelible. And
if I reckon correctly, there are five. The sacraments: properly
speaking the sacraments of consecration, of inauguration, the
start of a movement, an entry into life, into a state of life,
the sacraments of beginning. A registration. All of which are
indelible.

One of the marks of Christianity, historical, mystical and
indelible too, one of its essential characteristics is that these in-
scriptions are eternal; the register once opened is never closed,
not in all eternity. That is the master idea of Christianity, and
how perfectly married to reality it is, how well it conforms and
answers to reality, how strong the taste of reality, my child,
the feeling of growing old, of *my* growing old, of my *vieillissement,* my child, my dear child, though one must have passed
forty, as we have, you and I, you no doubt, and I without a
shadow of doubt, to know and taste it to the full. A register
once opened is never again closed; what is inscribed can never
be erased; there are no india rubbers, no *deletes,* as in your

typography; just two words: Charles, Péguy; your surname and Christian name; the name of your patron and the name of your father; the name of Borromeo and the name of your father who was a carpenter; the name of Borromeo, who was a sort of parish priest, like your Pope today, like your present Pope, a Bishop, an Archbishop; the name of your father who was a poor honest man, member of the parish, hardly a believer, like most Frenchmen in his day; the name of that great saint and the name of your father (temporally), dead so young, when you were barely born; formally, officially not a believer, not one of the faithful, in the eyes of the curés; deeply, really faithful, like all the Frenchmen of that time; and then there is Pierre, but it is not your *usual* Christian name. Those names on God's register are not effaced.

The Christian idea is that there are entries which admit of no exit; that one is not joking; that one is not playing ducks and drakes with everything, no matter what; that there are re-commencements, renewals (*de plano, de novo*) which cannot be attempted; that generally speaking the entry into certain states is definite; that a very large number of vocations, of destinations and resolutions, are irrevocable. How utterly opposed that idea is, my friend, to the frivolity of modern times, which claims to begin everything over again! How opposed that great idea is, that central Christian idea, and the whole theory and practice of the Christian, how utterly opposed to the frivolity of modern times, to the vanity and pretense that everything can be begun over again, when one likes, as one likes, to suit taste and fancy, folly and passion, which thinks everything can be remade, marriage in particular (it is marriage that shows it up best, because the instance is so glar-

ing!). So that the modern world, my friend, only wants to repeat, begin again, reverse the irreversible. And of the two, my
friend, which is right, in the detail of temporal life, I mean, in
everyday life, in experience and without invoking the help of
lawyers; alas, alas, my friend, one does not have to be forty,
like you, or to have forty centuries behind one, like me, to be
in any doubt. How can one doubt that the irreversible cannot
be reversed?

The five sacraments are in a sense the real sacraments, the
sacraments of inauguration, forming a family apart, clearly
marked, in the great family of sacraments. There must after all
be two families, since the first two, the sacraments of nourishment (both carnal and mystical) and the sacrament of purgation, are prescribed by rule, more or less canonical, and we are
recommended to multiply them. Whereas the other five are
not, may not be, repeated. The difference of technique reveals,
obviously, I would not say a different, but a double family.
The first two appertaining to nourishment (the second being
a preparation for food), both mystical and carnal. The others
being initiations, sacramental beginnings. Baptism marks and
sanctions our entry into the Christian life, the Christian city,
the Christian state; confirmation marks our entry into com-
merce with the Holy Spirit; Holy Orders mark our entry into
the sacerdotal state; matrimony marks our entry into the state
of marriage; and one might almost say into a *ménage* — you
know, my friend, young men knew almost as much about marriage in those days as your friend, Léon Blum. And finally
the sacrament of extreme unction which marks the entry into
the state of death, a unique preparation for death and judgment. So that it is easy to see that the viaticum, which is al-

most an eighth sacrament, comes punctually and exactly at the intersection of the two families, when it accompanies extreme unction; for if you like, it is a sacrament of nourishment, as before, but at the same time, seen from another angle, it is in the line of unique sacraments, and even occupies an eminent place among them, being itself eminent, and then occupying a singular place, at the end of the series, being the last of the seven or eight.

It is a great event for every man, even on his bed, to go his way for the last time, to see the sun for the last time. And never again. It was a great event even for my pagans, who were only shades hereafter. What is it not for you, for you Christians, my child? A terrible departure for you who pass immediately to judgment, who depart to fall under judgment.

Thus at one and the same time you forfeit the taste of bread and the color of the sun, everything to my pagans, a truly terrible event, but nothing for you Christians, which should be nothing for you, my poor children, nothing officially, formally, my poor dear children; but terrible for you too, because the body resists, the body revolts; terrible for you too, to forfeit the taste of bread and the color of the sun, the carnal sun, the earth's sun; for you too, my children, have carnal eyes, earthly eyes. And at the same time, my dear children, you are summoned to appear. Really you are overwhelmed. For both are terrible things. Not only do you leave our mother the earth, like the pagans; but on your journey you are at once summoned to appear before your judge. *Rex tremendae majestatis.* A truly terrible departure, and an arrival more terrible still.

How great is your need of the viaticum upon that journey.

Quantus tremor est futurus
Quando Judex est venturus
Cuncta stricte discussurus!

Quid sum miser tunc dicturus,
Quem patronum rogaturus,
Cum vix jestus sit securus?

O light of the day, as the ancients said,
O sun I see thee for the last time.
Sun,

said (our) Phèdre and yours, who knew what she was saying,
since she was descended from it,

Sun, I come to see thee for the last time:

But you are doubly tried. At the same instant, the same *momentum* (*momentum, movimentum,* that which moves, sets in
motion), at the same moment you have a twofold trial; and
what heart can withstand it? You have both one and the other.

You die like all of us. You die the old death like everyone
else, which is hard enough, the old death that is always new
(for while it is known to man, it is new to each and every one
of us). And not only in a certain egoistic sense, a natural sense,
not only is his own death always new to a man, but also and
perhaps more, which is to his honor, the death of friend, and
father and mother and child is always new to him. Humanity
is accustomed to death. But no man is accustomed to death, to
any death that touches him closely or even distantly, and even
perhaps if it does not touch him. For there is a residue of mystery in death, a center, an abyss, a revelation of mystery — and

quite independent of whose death, be it your father or your mother — every man is gripped. The most talkative are silent, excepting one that I know, and the most stupid, excepting one that I know, are silent, and the orators, though they, too, are stupid, are silent, and the deafest hear, and the blindest see, and the closed are opened and even those who are armored in insensibility bow their heads for a moment at a funeral.

Well, you all undergo that common death, my friend, and it is difficult enough to swallow; it is a terrible undertaking to die. I have seen a lot of men die, my child, I am very old. I am like an old doctor, trained to it and in practice. One submits: but one does not, my child, get accustomed to it. One only makes the pretense. You should know that it is always, without exception, a terrible undertaking, for all men, a terrible thing to renounce the light of day. How great must misery be for there to be so many men who go to meet that terrible death, who judge and declare it to be the lesser misery! Not just in words but in deed. What must their distress be! For carnal death, child, the separation and tearing asunder of the body, is an unbelievable distress, a terrible undertaking. And even of those who go to meet death there is not one who has not felt the blow. The saints themselves, my child, the greatest saints (in a sense even more than others), all felt the blow. St. Louis at Tunis, in the colony of Tunis. Perhaps more than others, more than carnal men. For the body defends itself, rebels and wants to know nothing about it. The mortal body refuses to know mortality. We often tell the perishable body in our literature that it is perishable. And it says nothing to the contrary, because it says nothing, being a silent young man, who is not "in" literature, who does no literary work. But when it is a question of death for good, death that is no longer a literary affair, when it's a matter of death, the body understands very well that it is no joking matter. It is warned by a deep instinct, that it's a matter of death. For ever. And then, well, the body rebels. It struggles to defend itself. It's not just. Organically just. And the body of the saint rebels no less than the body of the sinner. Perhaps more, in a certain sense. St. Louis at Tunis and Joan of Arc at Rouen. How could they not have felt the blow? Were their bodies not like ours? If they had not had bodies like ours they would not have been saints. They would have been angels. And one must understand Pascal's words literally, rigorously. "*Qui veut faire l'ange.*" How should they not have felt it, when God himself felt it? When Jesus, the first of saints, the first of your saints (*aliorum sanctorum*), felt it? St. Louis at Tunis and Joan of Arc at Rouen; Jesus on the Mount of Olives. The saint on his deathbed; the saint on her death pyre; Christ on the Mount of Olives.

If Jesus had not had a body, my child, he would have been an angel or he would have remained God, God only, and he would not have become man, a man like us. *God himself feared death.* A revolt against the plague; a revolt against the flames; a revolt against the crucifixion; always a carnal revolt. You, who read the Office of Good Friday, pay little enough heed. To you it is almost Easter, a preparation for Easter and the bells of Easter are already sounding in your imagination. It is not Good Friday, but the day before the vigil of Easter. Friday is always the day before the day before Sunday. That at least is what people think. And on Friday one is already thinking of Sunday. One is almost there. You read, you even sing the office of the dead, that Friday office, but you are not present.

You sing without attending. You barely hear that terrible commemoration of a frightful agony. You Christians, you sinners, don't care over much. The spring is coming. And at the very beginning of that week, inaugurating that week, there has just been the feast of spring, the Sunday of branches and trees, of flowers in bud, those carnal vegetables, the promises pushing forth, Palm Sunday, the feast of the sacred wood, the pagan wood, the Jewish feast (pagan and Jewish, those two great preparations for the feast of the Christian mystery). Eight days only, before the Sunday of Easter. The entry into Jerusalem only eight days before the entry into the Resurrection and into Eternal Life. The palms and the she-ass only eight days before the Resurrection of the crucified. *Easter in flower,* flowering Easter, only eight days before the Easter of mystical fruits. Fruitfulness accelerated, ripening so rapidly, in haste to mature, harvest almost instantaneous, early harvest, barns soon full, the *vendages* completed, the cellars full, the granaries well stacked.

Twenty centuries of Christians, two thousand generations of Christians, have rejoiced on Palm Sunday and at Easter. The joy of spring joining the joy of the Resurrection; the joy of the renaissance, temporal, carnal, mysterious, invading the joy of the great mystical Renaissance, the second birth, the survival. And the joy of Palm Sunday overflowing into the joy of Easter, stifling the despairing call of the Just One.

You feel that a work is being done for you. You know for certain that it is for your good; that the infinite agony of the Just One, that unequalled suffering and the despairing cry, is exactly what was needed to counterbalance the atrocious burden. You feel and know that that was precisely what was wanting to make up the infinite merit and compensate for that heavy load. You feel it is good for you; very good for you; a thoroughly good thing; that it is just what we needed; what our infirmity needed; a treasure of merit, of virtues. That treasure required the despairing call of the Just One. As it should be. We do not find it disagreeable. At all. An obscure and deep instinct, deeper even than our instinct for self-preservation, warns us obscurely, invincibly, that that is what saves us, that no less was needed, that that is the source of our salvation. And that operation (that passion and crucifixion) seems to us a sound operation, advantageous. We see that it is good. We are deeply reassured, in our bellies, in our carnal bellies. And it brings with it a certain sense of ease. That terrible dread, that giddiness and anguish, that metaphysical anxiety, that religious dread, which gripped our bellies, gripped our inwards, seized us in the pit of the stomach, is diminished and somewhat alleviated. And so we are disposed to look upon that tragic agony with a favorable eye. We have the courage to support, very courageously, the sufferings of others. And manifesting that courage, we support the sufferings of Jesus Christ with endless courage. We accept them with disarming naïveté, with a really disarming cruelty. All the naïve cruelty of the children of men comes into play. And what is more, what is best of all, my friend, that naïveté, that natural cruelty, is also our greatness in our misery (mutually and reciprocally), and one has also to say that it is this (this cruelty and egoism and this sort of insolence, this metaphysical and religious egoism) which perhaps constitutes the greatest act of faith that we have ever made, that we have ever signed; the most profound one too.

But next time you are ill, which is bound to happen with all your worry and work and your responsibilities, when next you fall sick, and are in bed, and you *have* what the doctors call neurasthenia, which is not an illness really, but a certain state in which we plumb our infirmity and misery, contemplate our distress and debility, in which we savor to the full our dread and our fate, and when nothing masks disappointing reality, when all the draperies and veils have fallen and truth is really naked as it is in those moments when we no longer lie, or disguise anything, and we no longer cheat, when in fact nothing subsists any longer but the sentiment of our nothingness, when we stop being crude and coarse (for coarseness, my friend, a certain crudeness, thickness of skin, undeniably gives us the strength to bear the shocks of life), then I do not advise you, my poor child, I do not advise you to refer to the text, as my historians say, to open your heart to that tragic agony, to that infinite distress. No, my friend. Never read that text, that *history,* which we put up with so easily. Stick to the interpreters.

O fils le plus aimé qui montait vers son père. Do not at that moment open the Gospel according to Matthew. All the rest was nothing, my friend: the soldiers, the prison, the tribunal, the crowds, Caiaphas and Pilate and Barabbas: *sub Pontio Pilato passus,* the crown of thorns, the flagellation, the way of the cross; Jesus falls for the third time; the thirst and the lance, the sponge and the vinegar: all that my friend, was as nothing. What was worse was the triple denial of Peter, and, worse still, no doubt, the betrayal of Judas, the kiss and the thirty pieces of silver. But all that was as nothing. This is what counted, the marrow of the suffering, the interior suffering of that passion:

Et assumpto Petro, et duobus filiis Zebediaei, coepit contristari, et moestus esse. XXVI, 37. *And taking with him Peter and the two sons of Zebedee, he began to grow sorrowful and to be sad.* And in this edition the page heading is *Tristitia et Oratio Christi: Then he saith to them: My soul is sorrowful even unto death; stay you here and watch with me.* You know, my friend, how they watched. But what you must observe, what is here announced, beside which all the rest is really nothing but procedure, is the marrow and content of the passion, is death itself, child, not an extraordinary death, but common death, pagan death, made infinite like a Christian death, for it was the first Christian death. It was death, my child, carnal death, simple, corporal, temporal death, the death of his body, of his human body. *Tristis usque ad mortem.* Sorrowful unto death. Without it being possible to know in so dense a text whether it is the duration that is meant: until my death, up to the moment of my death; or whether, it means equally, indivisibly: mortal sorrow, which goes to death, which makes death.

Et progressus pusillum, procidit in faciem suam, orans et dicens: Pater mi, si possibile est, transeat a me calix iste, verum tamen non sicut ego volo, sed sicut tu.

My child, if we were not dulled and deadened and petrified by generations of catechism, by habit, by catechistic habit, who would not be moved, who would not be appalled by those lines, by those atrocious lines, by that terrifying prayer? When one thinks. Thus everything was prepared, from eternity, everything was prepared. And behold. The whole of Christianity was ready. It had even been set in motion. He himself had set the tragic operation in motion. Temporally, eternally, everything was prepared. The mystery of the incarnation had taken place and already implied the mystery of the redemption. Everything was prepared. The thirty years of family life. The public life. The preaching and the parables on the mountainside and in the plains and on the lake of Tiberias. And now the crowning was about to begin. Everything was prepared. All the characters were ready on the boards to play their part in the drama. After years of intrigue, temporal years, of those intrigues customary among civil servants, my child (Romans, Romans, do you understand me), and it was under the Empire, Pontius Pilate had just been appointed Procurator in Judaea. It is so difficult to get a post. And Caiaphas, the prince of priests and scribes and senators, was High Priest.

Everything was prepared. He himself had put his hand to the work and given the last touches to the *foundation* of his city. The Church was founded. Peter was invested. The bread had been changed into the body, and the wine into blood, the wine of the grapes of the vine. What must death not be, my child, for him to have hesitated at that moment, for an atrocious hesitation to have disturbed his balance for an instant? He himself, the last, the prince of prophets, had prophesied his own death three or four times; had only recently foretold it. And now he was not only going to unsay all the prophets, but unsay himself. What must not death be, for its mere approach to have brought him to such a state? For make no mistake, my friend, that is what was at the heart of the passion.

And in that sense you will have realized that his passion, and above all his death, was as it were, the accomplishment and proof and verification, the concentration and the supreme realization of his incarnation; that the mystery of his passion, and above all, the mystery of his death, was at the same time the supreme realization of his incarnation. He saw death in full, and faced it in full, full-face. He was going to have to suffer death, death as in Villon, the death of all men, our common fate, the death of which your father died, your young father, when you were ten months old, the death your wife and children will suffer, one day. That carnal breach, that rupture of the tissues and of the blood vessels, and of all the lines and ligatures of life.

> La mort le fait frémir, pallir,
> Le nés courber, les vaines tendre,
> Le col enfler, la chaire mollir,
> Ioinctes et nerfs croistre et estendre.

> Pater mi, si possibile est transeat a me calix iste.

And by a wonderful inward accord he renews and recalls to memory the prayer which he had taught men, which he himself had invented at the time of his preaching. So that at the culmination of his distress, at the moment when he had most need for prayer, of the maximum of prayer, he rediscovered the very prayer which he had taught. *Pater noster qui est in coelis, sanctificetur nomen tuum; adveniat regnum tuum; fiat voluntas tua.* The echo rebounds, to that *fiat voluntas tua* spoken on the mountainside, rises up to that *fiat voluntas,* and by a secret interior rhythm, by a concordance of rhythm; to the first tradition of Genesis, to the *fiat lux* of the beginning of the world. And that reiterated form tautened, the repeated invocation drawn toward himself, *Pater mi* instead of *Pater noster,* drawing his father to him, produces such a confusion and penetration of the two persons, that in making that prayer one no longer knows, of a sudden, up to what point he is not suddenly speaking, very particularly, professionally almost, technically, as the Son of God.

XXVI, 43. *And he cometh again and findeth them sleeping: for their eyes were heavy. And leaving them he went again: and prayed the third time, saying the self-same words. And next at the ninth hour.* XXVII, 46. *Et circa horam nonam clamabit Jesus voce magna, dicens: Eli, Eli, lamma sabachthani?*

One must hope, my friend, one must believe that that double clamor, that unbelievable invocation, that reechoing cry, resounding from the Garden of Olives, echoing the three prayers, one must believe that that triple prayer meant no more, said no more, signified no more than carnal death, and the fear of carnal death: *My God, my God, why hast thou forsaken me?;* that that strange, incredible invocation does not mask or reveal, does not hide another fear, another death, that it does not reveal another mystery, a mystical mystery, infinitely more profound. Let us say that he had a body, and that his body defended itself well. His body revolted, rebelled in the face of death. He was man to the end. The body which had borne him for thirty and three years, the body which had received the *spirit* of God (*emisit spiritum*), the body which had carried that enormous burden, which had carried him during those days, Thursday and Friday, the body of man refused to yield. Like all human bodies it revolted against the death of the body. And he himself followed his body, in a certain sense (just as we sinners and as the saints often do), followed his body like a wretched man, the evocation of his body. Accomplishing and crowning in a wonderful way his incarnation in his redemption.

And yet he offered himself. You, too, suffer it. You, too, suffer that death, exactly like the ancients. Jesus conquered death, triumphed over death. Jesus rose again from the dead. But you, you must suffer carnal death as before. Like all those who went before, like the Greeks and the Jews, the sages and the prophets, the heroes and the Maccabees. There is no way of avoiding it. If you had succeeded, if you Christians had not suffered death, everyone would have known it, it would have been too obvious. You alone of all the beasts of the earth, of all living things — it would have been a miracle, a scandal. It would have caused a tumult. Everyone would have rushed and wanted to join you. Whereas everything in your organization is so arranged as to have the contrary result. How would all those people, my dear Gide, how would they all have passed through the narrow gate? In your mechanism, your *mystique,* everything is so arranged that it really should be the narrow gate, so that the passage should be bristling with difficulties of all kinds, so that few should pass, and at the cost of a thousand difficulties; the small number of the elect. That is one more proof of the capital importance of death in your economy. That dreadful passage, that terrible experience. And thus the religion of eternal life is not the religion of life immortal, by which I mean that it was not founded as a religion of terrestrial immortality, corporal, carnal, temporal immortality.

Fiat lux; verum tamen non sicut ego volo, sed sicut tu. Fiat voluntas tua. At a distance of fifty centuries, from before Adam, till the new Adam, the same words echo, and at an interval of more than fifty centuries the cry of the second creation echoes and answers the words of the first creation: faithful echo, following the same movement, the same rhythm of life. And as grammar requires, subjunctive answers subjunctive; and God after more than fifty centuries, answers God.

On the threshold of the first creation, in the beginning, (an) active God pronounced the authoritative word, the word of command, of creation, an active, effective word. On the threshold of the second creation (a) humble God faithfully echoed the humble words of submission. Of the Passion. There, Christians, is your progress; there is progress for you, real progress, religious progress. That is what it consists in. The form is given by the echo. *Lux fiat. Voluntas fiat.* In the beginning, a God in all his glory, in the glory of his power, in the (young) majesty of his creation; and more than fifty centuries after, after more than fifty centuries of progress, a God prostrate upon the ground, *procidit in faciem suam*, a God fallen upon his face, on the earth, humble, humbled, in the humbleness of man. There, my child, is your progress. Such is its form: its marvellous, singular form. A failure in the eyes of men. A decline. And that is what you call progress. Confess, my child, admit that it is not progress according to Condillac, nor according to your French eighteenth century.

Yours, too, is the religion of progress; but what progress!

Fiat lux, fiat voluntas. And just as the first creation was the creation of the whole world, *totius orbis universi*, of the whole creation, that faithful echo was no less exactly the creation of the spiritual, the proper creation of the spiritual world delayed for more than fifty centuries.

Everything was waiting. The lance and the nails, nature and the miracle, the order of nature and the order of the miracle. The sacrifice was waiting. Just as the stone was waiting for the victim in the sacrifice of Isaac. But no angel came to avert the blow from the new victim; no angel came from heaven. And on that point, contrary to what is usually held, the new law showed itself more severe than the old: more exacting, more sanguinary, more avid of blood and of what blood! The sacrifice was waiting, the sacrifice which only happened once, which only could happen once (which has happened, which has been consummated hundreds and thousands of times, which is consummated every day, which will be consummated eternally). He took time and in his very obedience he trembled one instant on the balance.

Oh, no, my child, that was not historical progress. I know too much about it.

That will was done. Light was made. It was made in him; and singularly enough it is made again in you, in each of you *singulis vestris*. In you, my children. That will to death, to natural, temporal death. Otherwise, if there were the least exception, your whole system would be knocked sideways, flat, and people would take it poorly, as they say.

Madame l'Histoire, with all due respect you talk like a *cantinière*.

My child, that is because I have had a lot to do with soldiers.

I doubt it, *Madame l'Histoire*, I doubt it.

My child, it's the fault of your curriculum, the old one, in which military history occupied an enormous amount of space, whole volumes. Yes, yes, it occupied (and she went on chewing her gums, her almost toothless old gums) a disproportionate amount of space. As everyone now knows, as we have since discovered, as all the young men have discovered: soldiers and war never played any part in the history of humanity. Indeed, it took up too much space.

In fact, she did not really talk like a *cantinière*, and when she began to speak of sacred things, which at heart she was drawn to, she softened, she was moved. "But do not fret," she said to me, "do not worry, the young men I see nowadays will soon teach me their measured, refined language, and I shall end by becoming a Doctor of History. My sister Thalia is already a Doctor of Letters. All I meant was that otherwise your whole system would be ill received and would fall flat. There must be no exception. Otherwise the whole thing collapses, and one could go in through wide-open doors. Exactly the opposite, in fact, of what was intended."

For your whole apparatus is built and *founded* on there being a risk; a total risk; man must make his choice in absolute freedom. There must therefore, in the last analysis, be a risk; one always comes back to the bet. If you cut out anything, my friend, any of man's miseries, sickness, poverty, death, all would be lost, everything would collapse. For then the whole world would want to enter, and there would be a rush. An appalling rush, a crowd. If there were any escape, above all, escape from death, my child, God could never have known his own. Such is the price of death. There had to be that risk and everything had to remain as it was, so that in the last analysis everything comes back to a risk, a gamble. The risk must be preserved, integrally. That, my child, is Christianity.

In order that man should and because, in the last analysis, man had to choose and pronounce himself freely, in all freedom. In a state of complete equilibrium, so to speak, as before, on the razor edge of freedom. That is why Christianity has never had, never could have (it would be senseless, and one even asks oneself what it could mean) proofs, has never brought proofs forward, in the coarse sense which people give to that word, that is to say, proofs which prove rigorously, logically; and it never could bring proofs. On the contrary, everything is foreseen, prepared, for it not to bring proofs, for it never to bring proofs, so that proofs should not have any meaning whatsoever. Until the Day of Judgment, when they will no longer be necessary. Its best proof, its only proof, is not to offer proofs. That is one of your Christian arrangements. And it only seems curious to coarse-grained people, to reasoners, I mean.

If by some misfortune it were *proved*, as they say, by demonstrative reasons, logical reasons, if it had supplied rigorous proof, everything would collapse. For all the reasoners, and they are legion (for they are the vast majority, and they are much more numerous than the sensual and the luxurious), all the coarse-grained would have been compelled, logically, to enter in. And liberty, once again, falls to the ground. And again it collapses if a single human misery is spared you. (The total liberty of man must have had an infinite price in that affair of yours, and obviously, quite obviously, the intention was that everything should be done out of love in your system, and that love should only move in a full, complete and well-balanced liberty.) Otherwise everything falls to the ground, the price falls, and everything is lowered and degraded, for if you were spared any of man's miseries the gamble would be a sham, there would be nothing to stake. But don't worry, my friend, the stake is there all right, and if anything you have been too well served. You have been given good measure. Historically one can almost recognize a Christian, a good Christian, from the fact that he is tried with endless worries. One might almost suppose they had fallen off on one side to make quite sure of not falling off on the other. Really, liberty, man's freedom, must be infinitely precious. It plays such an essential part in your *mystique*.

There is a certain conformity, a secret wish, a singular preference, a certain complicity and understanding between you and misery, an inward secret taste that betrays you, and which would allow the historian to follow your traces, if he were awake. That, too, is why humanity as a whole has not, alas, changed noticeably since Jesus. Fortunately for you it has not. Since the coming and the death of Jesus, my child, who came to save the world. Since his birth and nativity, incarnation and redemption, since lance and cross. After so many miseries the world, as anyone can see, has not changed. Since that unique history, which should have renewed the world (no, not renewed, but saved, which strictly speaking has a totally different meaning), since then the world has not changed noticeably. I mean on the face of it, superficially, publicly, and historically. I mean, more exactly, to the vulgar gaze, to the temporal material, the public eye, the historical glance. As previously, there have been wars.

The Christian, Christianity, Christendom, is not a public operation, a superficial, historical operation; it is not a public event. It is a secret event, a profound, inward operation, and often, the more profound it is the less it modifies external aspects and appearances. After as before there have been terrible misfortunes, plagues as bad as the plague of Athens, dreadful wars, hatreds, impurities; man has hated and massacred man. The Christian, Christianity, is a molecular operation which often leaves the skin intact. One is tempted to think

they have fallen, almost deliberately, on the side of extrava-
gance to make quite sure of not falling on the side of avarice,
or avariciousness. Avariciousness with misfortune.

The calculation has been crowned with success; it has succeeded so well that one might almost say that it has turned
back upon its author. The Christian world has been so inun-
dated with misfortunes that it no longer looks natural; it is
suspect; it becomes a proof. Here once again the trials accumulate to become a proof: the proof is that the Christian is
proved and tried. But Christianity is not made for those who
want proofs. But for the opposite. For those who want to be
proved.

My friend, if humanity in general had changed as from a
certain date, if suddenly, instantaneously, automatically almost, it had become infinitely different, it would have been
known. That would have constituted a proof: a complete
proof. The most stupid would have seen it. The historians
(even) would have perceived it. The chroniclers, the chronolo-
gists, the chronographers, would have intercepted the date
and got it down on their tablets. Whereas in fact no one knows
it, either in the primary schools or in the universities. It would
have constituted a proof one could put into books, into exams.
Suitable for public meetings. But none were wanted. All that
was wanted was the secret proof which by a singular mystery,
by an evident contradiction, seizes men one by one, *singulos
homines,* as though by a miracle, by some miraculous contradiction, one by one, and yet at the same time from above and
below, seizes them instantaneously, in communion. A subterranean, and to use the right word, a sly and slippery proof,
that seizes a man's roots; by the roots, by the belly and by

his heart; and by a very strange contradiction seizes and vanquishes him in isolation, face to face with those formidable proofs, yet wholly and entirely in communion.

The perennial life of the Church throughout those twenty centuries is by itself proof enough, is almost too much (the moderns themselves would have rushed in precipitously, though one must say that a lot has been done to keep the moderns, in particular, away); that sort of temporal eternity of the Church, that perpetuity throughout twenty centuries, particularly of its government, its most detestable government, the political, I mean (temporal and often spiritual, temporal always and spiritual often enough), of its government, its *politique* — that perpetuity is really too much, with its twenty centuries already acquired, offering almost too spectacular a proof, really too blinding, too crude, too coarse for books, too easy to fit into university and ecclesiastical disciplines, to fit into a school program; something one can quote. God will really have to be careful and take precautions, so that, with time, the temporal perpetuity of the Church which is bound to grow scandalously, should not form too formal an argument; even cruder than it is today; too obvious; too highly colored; in such bad taste; after thirty or forty or fifty centuries that crude proof will certainly need to be balanced by a contingent of scandals in proportion. Otherwise there would be no liberty for man (we have so little as it is). And it is no doubt as a safeguard, and for the sake of preserving that little bit of freedom, that we have the triumphant scandal of the modern world.

Thus the communion has followed man (but has followed him at the same time from within, so to speak, and even strictly speaking, from ahead); Christianity follows the Christian; Christendom follows the fate of the Christian. And just as the Christian era did not open an era of happiness, worldly happiness, for the Christian man, far from it, so too the Christian era did not inaugurate an era of happiness for humanity as a whole. Far from it. Jesus did not come to create powerful authorities, men with power, in this world. He said it often enough. In enough different forms. He succeeded only too well, so to speak. Thus the spectacle of humanity considered as a spectacle, as a historical spectacle, crudely considered, is, if anything, rather worse after than before, unfortunately much worse: sadder, uglier. At least we say that because we do not know, or know properly, the miseries of the ancient world, the ancient miseries, and because we think we know the Christian world. Bad enough anyhow, for it to be, if people knew how to use their eyes, a historical proof, a sort of counterproof, a striking counterproof.

Yes, if people knew how to look, you would be given away by the quality of your misery. Not given away by the sort of proof you require, one of those indecent, shameful proofs which catch you unawares, seize you in your isolation, one of those secret, supposedly individual and hidden proofs; but revealed, on the contrary, by one of the proofs that we historians ourselves can appreciate, crude and formal, superficial and solid, for after all, one must be fair to everyone — in fact, by a historical proof. For the spectacle has changed greatly with your new era, your Christian era; and it has changed very much for the worse.

Not only have you had more crimes, it seems (to me); but

more *ennuis,* more worries. You are penetrated and soaked in *ennui* as never before. Assailed by trials and troubles of every kind. And they all have a particular flavor, your shame and your crimes and your *ennui,* that *ennui* from which you never escape, has its own flavor. Your miseries have a taste all of their own. Christian misery properly so called. The worst of all. There, my child, is Christianity.

You have eternalized everything. You have grabbed all the values on the market. And turned them all into infinite values. And now one can no longer be sure of quiet for a single moment. There was trouble enough in coming to terms with purely human values. You see what Christianity is like. You have taken the simplest of all values, all the human values and made them divine. You take everything to God, everything back to God. You touch God on all sides. Touch him and wound him everywhere. You can no longer move. You have made a sin of everything; of the least of crimes. And the least of your sins touches God; it not only touches Jesus in his glory; it becomes an accomplice of the Roman lance, touches the mortal body of Jesus, his suffering body, wounding it in the side during his passion, his torture. Such extremes, my child, make life impossible. Such horrors, my child, as I, history, have never had to register, such as I have never known, such confusion, such complicity, such a communion makes life unlivable. Saints, great saints, many of the greatest, remained their whole life long prostrate in insurmountable suffering, prostrate with horror. And one asks oneself, I often ask myself, how you can live. Nature, carnal nature, which lies beneath, must have retained an immense power, an instinct

of self-preservation, a will to live and not to die. But in order
to have achieved that compensatory power, the grace of God
must have been infinite and the merits of Christ infinite.

It is very remarkable, to me, history, from one point of view,
from a purely historical point of view, and speaking historically, that the two highest cultures that humanity has ever
known, the two old cultures, I mean, both infinitely superior
to the modern (one cannot really say modern culture), superior to everything modern, the pagan and the Christian,
should both equally have been, each according to its type and
nature, *founded* upon misfortune; upon the consideration and
contemplation and meditation of misfortune. Upon a sort of
appropriation of misfortune. For you Christians, it is striking, piercing. To the point at which it forms a proof: one of
those, precisely, that ought not to have been given. But for
the ancients, what misfortune, child, what misfortune!

All that one can say is that in your case it is, as it were,
more specifically, more professionally, misery; and to them,
certainly, misfortune. That is one of the nuances I can still see
perfectly well. Péguy always seems to be saying that I am an
old idiot, and if he doesn't say it always, then if I know how
to read, he writes it often enough (though he is sure to say
I don't know how to read), which is in a way more serious.
Well, then, idiotic as I am, there you have some of the lessons
which I can still draw from my experience, some of the lessons I have drawn, and continue to draw from the history of
humanity, some of the nuances that my poor old aged eyes,
weak from use, can still distinguish. You Christians *go in for*

misery, you make misery. And the pagans, above all, go in for misfortune. A sad distribution indeed, a sad settlement, a sad setting forth, sorry specializations you have made between you. As if there were not enough for everyone. You only had to choose and cut into that sorrow, into the common domain of the infirmities of common, of sorry humanity. And the only difference between you would have been that you would have leaned a little more to this side, and they would have leaned a little more to that side. Oh, you were only embarrassed by the choice: you two, the greatest, the highest, the only two great cultures that the world has ever known. You divided sad humanity between you: you divided its miseries.

There were plenty more, plenty to choose from for some amateur of common miseries.

In your case, Christians, it is striking, flagrant, scandalous. I meant that it is a scandal, speaking technically, that it causes scandal. In a word, it is demonstrative. But for the ancients, the great ancients . . .

This book is set in 11 on 14 Fournier, a typeface
produced in about 1740 by Pierre Simon Fournier,
the Parisian typefounder and engraver, inventor of
the typographic point and author of *Manuel Typographique*.
The typeface was recut in 1925 by the Monotype design
staff, under the direction of Stanley Morison, as part of a
program of making historic typefaces once more available.

Printed on paper that is acid-free
and meets the requirements of the American National
Standard for Permanence of Paper for Printed
Library Materials, z39.48-1992. ⊗

Book design by Erin Kirk New,
Athens, Georgia
Typography by Tseng Information Systems, Inc.,
Durham, North Carolina
Printed and bound by Sheridan Books, Inc.,
Chelsea, Michigan